Praise for *The Customer Comes Second:*

"Hal Rosenbluth's story is one of the great, unsung business success sagas of the '80s and '90s. And it is one that explains why most other customer service programs bomb. Put your frontline employees first, if you're serious about putting your customers first. It's a wonderful message."

−TOM PETERS

"If you can't quit your job and work for Hal Rosenbluth, at least read his book."

−MICHAEL LORELLI
Division President, PepsiCo

"The *way* we treat those who work for us has everything to do with *how* they work for us. Rosenbluth and Peters's book squarely proves what goes around comes around."

−HARVEY MACKAY

"Hal Rosenbluth is a future visionary for American management: He shows how to combine American business with heart."

−FAITH POPCORN
Chairman, BrainReserve
Author, *The Popcorn Report*

"Hal Rosenbluth's message, like his style, is deceptively simple and seductive to the sensitive and caring leader. This should be required text for future professional service firm leaders."

−IRA M. ROSENMERTZ
Managing Director, Arthur Andersen & Co.

"Hal practices what he has written in this book and so do his people."

−PHIL LIPPINCOTT
Chairman and CEO, Scott Worldwide

D0196997

"It was high time for someone to write down some of the common-sense axioms that we 'people believers' hold so dear. Hal has done that in an admirable way."

—GEORGE W. EBRIGHT
Chairman and CEO, Cytogen

"Hal has built a championship team and his creative game plan can make every executive a winner!"

—STEVE SABOL
President, NFL Films

"I know few executives who have done as well managing a growth cor-poration through difficult and rapidly changing times. Part of Rosenbluth International's success comes from Hal's managerial skill and vision; much of it comes from his skill in encouraging his employ-ees to contribute their own vision. Both are described in this book."

—ERIC CLEMONS
Associate Professor of Decision Sciences
The Wharton School of Business

"Hal Rosenbluth's energetic style and creative approach make this book a joy to read. . . . Hal's ideas are fresh, exciting, innovative–and they can work for you."

—U.S. SENATOR KENT CONRAD

"*The Customer Comes Second* captures a key to Rosenbluth's success, and that is when you put your internal customer (his employees) first, you have accomplished a competitive edge that few companies ever achieve."

—R. H. THURMAN
Executive Vice-President, Rhone-Poulenc Rorer, Inc.
President, Rhone-Poulenc Rorer Pharmaceuticals

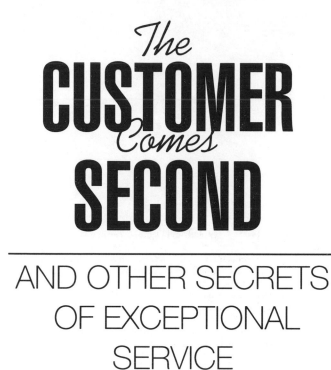

The
CUSTOMER
Comes
SECOND

AND OTHER SECRETS
OF EXCEPTIONAL
SERVICE

Hal F. Rosenbluth *and*
Diane McFerrin Peters

Quill
William Morrow
New York

It is the policy of William Morrow and Company, Inc., and its imprints and affiliates, recognizing the importance of preserving what has been written, to print the books we publish on acid-free paper, and we exert our best efforts to that end.

Library of Congress Cataloging-in-Publication Data

Rosenbluth, Hal.
THE CUSTOMER COMES SECOND: AND OTHER SECRETS OF EXCEPTION-
AL SERVICE / Hal Rosenbluth and Diane McFerrin Peters.
   p. cm.
   ISBN 0-688-13246-4
   1.Travel agents—Management. I. Peters, Diane McFerrin.
II. Title.
G154.R67   1992
338.4'791—dc20   91-44027
                                                   CIP

Printed in the United States of America

13   14   15

BOOK DESIGN BY PATRICE FODERO

*In dedication
to the associates of Rosenbluth Inc.
and our clients
who inspire us to provide service from our
hearts*

CONTENTS

CHAPTER 1

CULTURAL METAMORPHOSIS

A LOOK INTO THE FUTURE

Just a brief decade and a half ago, we were like most companies. Back then, if someone had described our company to me as it is today, I would have thought they were crazy. I also would have given just about anything to work here.

A lot has happened; much of it by accident, some by design. But lately the transformations our company has gone through are being studied and written about everywhere. We didn't solicit the curiosity and attention, but we found ourselves in the middle of it, and we've been presented with this opportunity to share the steps of our inadvertent journey.

When news spread of our company's 7,500-percent growth in revenue over the past fifteen years (from $20 million to $1.5 billion while maintaining profitability above industry standards), we began to be literally inundated with requests to share our "secret" of success.

Our secret is controversial. It centers around our basic

belief that *companies must put their people—not their customers—first.*

You might wonder how our clients feel about this. For our people, the clients are priority number one. Our company has built a solid reputation in the field of customer service (in fact, our client retention rate is 96 percent), but we have actually done it by focusing inside, on our own people.

Companies have profound and far-reaching effects on the lives of the people who work for them, so it becomes the obligation of companies to make the effects positive. All too often companies bring stress, fear, and frustration to their people—feelings they bring home with them each night. This creates problems at home which people bring back to work in the morning. The cycle is both terrible and typical, but not what most companies would want as their legacy. It's certainly not what our company wants: especially when there are so many things we can all do to enrich the lives of our people.

If this all sounds simple, it's not. Let's take a look at where we came from, where we are today, and just how we got there. Here begins the charting of a road map for change.

LONG, LONG AGO . . .

Our company began a century ago as a forerunner to travel agencies as we know them today. My great-grandfather, Marcus Rosenbluth, founded the company in 1892 to provide transportation for immigrants from Europe to the United States via steamship.

It was a full-service business. The company acted as a bank to help families save for the fifty-dollar ticket. Because he spoke nine languages, Marcus was able to help sort out the immigration paperwork and facilitate the process of reuniting families. Through the network he built, he even helped immigrants find work in their new country.

THE SEEDS OF CHANGE

The company survived the astronomical changes in the world around it and thrived. Some eighty-two years after its founding, Rosenbluth was firmly entrenched as the largest and strongest travel agency in the Philadelphia area. The firm's success was indisputable. Then I joined the firm, hell-bent on changing it from head to toe.

I admit, I didn't want to join the family business in the first place, which probably made me look at it with an unusually harsh eye. What I saw was a flourishing business held back by politics; powerful individual efforts thwarted by a lack of teamwork. This was an environment I didn't relish working in, so it was likely many of my colleagues didn't like it much either.

Change has to start somewhere, and here it began with a group of mavericks who pioneered our corporate travel department, at the time a low-profile start-up unit. Today it makes up over 90 percent of our company's operations.

Prior to airline deregulation there was not much of a market for corporate travel services. But when fares and schedules began to change by the minute in the new deregulated environment, corporations saw the impact business travel could have on their lives and their bottom lines. That's when corporate travel management skyrocketed for us.

This budding operation wasn't a place for creatures of habit, lovers of the status quo. Every day meant change, a whirlwind of activity, a future unfolding by the minute. The nine-to-five routine became more like five (A.M.) to nine (P.M.) in this uncharted territory.

I was drawn to it instinctively, as though I were coming home. This was the perfect place for the transformation of our company to begin. I had no specific plan for the change but I wanted to capture the spirit I had found in this unsung department, a spirit of cooperation, friendship, fierce dedication, and hard work. I knew we had to concentrate, above all, on the people *providing* the service. From there, everything else would fall into place.

THE TURNING POINT

The changes began in our little corner of the company, and the turning point came when we put our people first. It didn't happen overnight. A sweeping change like that takes commitment, persistence, and time. People have to change and so do the infrastructure and systems that support them.

Such change can start as a grass roots movement. It can be embraced by top leadership and filter throughout an organization. Or, as in our case, it can take hold in one segment of a company and spread laterally. The only important thing is for it to start.

We're talking about a change that puts the people in organizations above everything else. They are cared for, valued, empowered, and motivated to care for their clients. When a company puts its people first, the results are spectacular. Their people are inspired to provide a level of service that truly comes from the heart. It can't be faked. The only way to emulate it is to create it from scratch.

When something this positive is set in motion, it gets noticed. It spreads. It's natural—compatible with the way we are supposed to live as human beings. No longer must we each be one person at home and another at work.

At Rosenbluth, these changes produced very tangible results in our underdog department, and company leaders took note. Everyone around us wanted to work in an environment like ours. Our people were happy, fulfilled, and excelling, and it showed. Clients enjoyed working with our people and they let us know it.

It was just a matter of time before, department by department, our entire organization was completely transformed. Today, people-first behavior permeates our company and impacts everything we do.

We begin by hiring the right kind of people, ones who will carry the torch. This emphasis extends to our training programs, which are as much philosophical as technical. It shapes our supplier relationships, our partnerships with our clients, and even positively affects our home lives. In fact, this is a way of life for us.

Focusing on our people is the foundation. The many other components that make up our company, the tools we utilize, and the theories by which we live all stem from this basic belief.

Just how we changed and the specific programs we put in place to help us make those transitions are explained in the coming chapters. We'll also take a look at the methods used to monitor our progress and the results we've attained along the way. But first, it might be helpful to know a little about us.

WHO ARE WE AND WHAT IN THE WORLD DO WE DO?

We are a global travel management firm that operates three primary lines of business with a fourth, a diversified services arm, under development. The three travel-related lines of business are leisure or "vacation" travel, meeting and motivation management (programs that motivate and inspire people to reach goals their company has set, most often with travel as the reward), and corporate travel.

Our most explosive growth has been in the corporate arena. By consolidating companies' business travel we help them to realize gains in time and money. We do this through purchasing power, information, efficiencies, and comprehensive services that begin before the travelers even plan their trips and continue long after their return.

Outside our industry, we're not a household name but our clients are. We are fortunate to count among them some of the most highly respected firms in the world, including 16 percent of the Fortune 50 companies. We manage the corporate travel accounts of over 1,600 corporations, and our client list is the envy of our industry. The firms we work with are clearly "best of class" in their respective industries.

There are over 2,600 people in our company in over 400 offices in 36 states, Europe, and the Orient. Our headquarters are in Philadelphia. At last count, our annual sales volume was over $1.5 billion and growing. Rosenbluth is a privately held company.

We didn't conduct any studies or create a plan for the changes we made in our company. We decided that as we grew from a regional to a global company we would need to formalize what we had captured, in order to retain and nurture it. So we began to look closely at the things we were doing and how we were doing them. From there, our theories took shape.

We've shared our philosophical and cultural training programs with a great many companies, which may surprise you. We've even set up a new line of business in order to be able to handle those requests.

Yet I hesitated, at first, when I thought about sharing our ideas in an open forum such as this—partly because I'm not overly comfortable doing so and partly out of concern about giving away competitive information. But I decided that what we have learned is too important not to share. Perhaps, by sharing what we have learned, we can help others to have similar results. The best part of all is that it's the right thing to do, the right way to lead. Everyone wins.

A PREVIEW OF THINGS TO COME

The pages that follow do not tell just the "story of our company." This is intended to be a reference manual of factors that contributed to one company's success, of ideas that can be borrowed, adapted, elaborated upon, customized, and improved for application to your business.

I have tried to create a reference you can turn to periodically to try some of the ideas in your company. They can be implemented either together or separately. It's not necessary to employ them all in order for any one idea to be effective. They are intended to be cherry-picked as you find appropriate.

With these ideas, we turned our organization upside down and achieved results we never dreamed of. Ours is the story of an old company doing new things. Companies can change. We are living proof. It is our conviction that companies *must* change. We have that obligation to our clients and the people we employ.

The ideas I've included cut across industry and country. They center around *people*, so they can apply to any business. I hope you will find them helpful for yours.

CHAPTER 2

HOW IT ALL BEGINS

Most people can't sleep the night before their first day of a new job. They probably decided two weeks in advance what they'd wear. They can't wait to get started, meet new people, see everything, do great things.

After all the anticipation, their first day is usually a big yawn. They find themselves hidden away in a room somewhere filling out forms. What a mistake! First impressions are lasting. Is that how most companies would like to be remembered? I doubt it. That's not the perception we'd like to create.

First days at our company are a little different. Every person who joins our team, regardless of position, department, level, location, or line of business, comes to our headquarters for the first two days of his or her career. Everyone participates in the same program together.

A lot of people never get to see their company's headquarters. They may never meet the top officers of the company. Here, they do both on day one. They also learn about what's really important in the company. And they have fun.

There are substantial benefits to this program. No doubt, it's a morale booster. It encourages buy-in from the start. It also prompts buy-out, which is important. Giving people an in-depth look at our culture lets them make a well-informed decision about whether or not this is the right place for them, and that helps us.

A new associate orientation program is a valuable tool to maintain culture as a company grows. Everyone gets the story straight. Everyone hears the same message. It starts people off on the right foot. It's really a tool from which all companies could benefit. I'll explain the way our program works.

New Associate Orientation is held each Monday and Tuesday, so everyone begins their employment on those days. The program is mandatory and no days should be worked prior to completing it.

On the first day, people get to know the other new associates who have joined the company that week. In the morning, they spend time in small groups, learning about each other. They become immersed in the company's philosophies and values and they begin to see their role in the future of our company. In the afternoon, the emphasis is on teamwork, perception, and listening skills.

People are always surprised to learn that they've been brought to headquarters just for philosophical training. Once we tell them how important these principles are to our company, they begin to see the emphasis we place on our values.

The second day is all about service. We focus on our clients and their needs and expectations. And we don't do it in a conventional way. In fact it borders on the bizarre.

Groups of four or five create the worst service experience they can think of. You can see the scowls on their faces as they start talking about all the terrible service episodes in their lives. You expect that at any minute, as in the movie *Network*, they'll stand up and say, "I'm mad as hell and I'm not going to take it anymore."

The groups decide which service experience is the worst and then embellish it, making it as ugly as it can be. They get to vent their frustrations by acting out the episode they dreamed up. Next, they return to their groups and make their service story a positive one, improving on it in every way they can imagine. Then they perform the good-service experiences in skits.

They expect that's all but it's not. Even the very best of service can be improved upon. So back to their groups they go to create superior service—elegant service. But the point is that it shouldn't even stop there. Service can be taken from bad to good and from good to exceptional, but there are infinite ways it can go beyond exceptional—and that's the range we're interested in.

Most of the skits wind up involving restaurants or travel. (That should tell us something about the perception of our industry.) People really let their imaginations run wild. One group created a "no frills" airline with no seats. Passengers were tied in with ropes and pushed out the door with parachutes instead of landing.

After the initial shock of having to get up in front of a bunch of people they hardly know, people usually become immersed in the experience. The skits are so realistic that once when a group was acting out a barroom brawl, a passerby called the police.

After the service skits, the group tours our resource and development center and corporate headquarters, stopping to meet as many individuals as possible. Then on to the culmination of the program, afternoon tea—with a twist. Our new associates are served by the top officers of the company.

There's a service message behind the choice of a tea for the activity. A cup of tea can come from a vending machine, it can be tossed to you in a diner, or can be elegantly served to you at a high tea. The tea is just a product; the service surrounding it makes all the difference in the world.

By serving our new associates, we're showing them that we're happy they're part of the team, they're important to us, and our people come first. We talk about what we believe in. We discuss what's on their minds. Nothing is off limits.

Once when I was serving tea, a new associate asked me how much money I make. I told him when it's a good year I make a lot and when it's a bad year I take it on the chin. Another asked me what I would do if I weren't CEO of Rosenbluth. I told her I'd like to be the Philly Phanatic because I'm a closet clown and I love baseball. But most of the questions are about the future of the company.

One point we make very clear is that it's *their* company now, and each time they begin a comment or question with "Your company . . ." I correct them and have them start again, saying, "Our company . . ." I think it's important for them to feel a sense of ownership from day one.

Starting Out Right
A *Summary*

- Training should begin with a formal orientation program, which every new person completes before beginning his or her first day at work. First impressions are lasting and both good and bad habits begin early. Everyone should go through the same program, regardless of the job or location.

CHAPTER 3

HAPPINESS IN THE WORKPLACE

Does the proverb "A picture is worth a thousand words" really ring true? On a hunch that it might, we instituted a program that has turned out to be one of the company's most memorable.

We sent a letter to one hundred associates asking them to draw a picture of what the company means to them. We enclosed construction paper and a box of crayons wrapped in ribbon.

Almost immediately, we began receiving people's drawings. The individuality of each was delightful. The company doesn't mean exactly the same thing to any two people. But there were some very common themes: happy faces; illustrations of service to clients and fellow associates; and lots and lots of salmon. (The salmon is a sort of mascot for us.)

That's all fine, but great value also comes from the *unhappy* pictures. There were five. We were glad to see that people felt free to submit negative drawings. The most important benefit of this program was that those drawings brought out problems we had been unaware of.

The most chilling drawing was on two pages. The first showed a family sitting around a fire, children playing, kittens and puppies. The picture was colorful, warm, and cozy. People were happy. I felt happy just looking at it. At the top it said, "BEFORE."

When I turned the page I was in for a rude awakening. The second sketch was in pencil. It was stark and cold. There was a person alone and shivering. The fire was out. The room was completely bare. I was horrified. At the top it said, "NOW."

I called and had a long talk with the artist and learned that an announcement had been made in her office that some of their work was being moved to another site. People there thought they were going to lose their jobs. In fact, plans had already been made for the people affected to be trained for a new function that was moving to their office. Unfortunately, *that* information wasn't shared with them.

I don't think I could have understood her feelings any better from a conversation than from those pictures. And I wonder if that conversation would have happened without the pictures.

We were also concerned about those who received the mailing but never responded to it, so we checked with each person. Not everyone feels comfortable drawing, and that's not a problem. But there were a few who hesitated to tell us what they thought, and that's a problem. So I talked with each of them to ensure their concerns were dispelled.

We learned so much from the program that we decided to extend it to our clients. We sent one hundred of them paper and crayons, and the response was overwhelming. One of the most interesting findings was the clear similarity between the drawings submitted by our clients and those done by our associates. It was especially fascinating to match up drawings from specific clients with the drawings of the associates who serve their account. It proved to be an effective gauge of happiness, service, perception, and communication.

Since our initial mailings we have repeated the program four times. Now, we receive unsolicited drawings on a weekly basis from associates and clients alike.

How Can We Be Serious About This?
The Basis for the People-First Philosophy

Companies must put their people first. Yes, even before their customers. There. Now I've said it. I know it's controversial. It makes most people nervous just to hear it, but it works.

Once we were conducting a site visit with a potential client, who visited a variety of departments in several of our offices. At the conclusion of the tour one of the company's executives actually asked if we were some sort of cult. Everyone was so happy he was skeptical. I know he was half-joking, but it struck home with us just how different we are. He decided he liked that, and the company is now our client.

On the surface, it all might sound like a lot of fluff—but this is serious stuff. When we first tell people what we're all about they usually look at us kind of funny, but as the saying goes, "The proof of the pudding is in the eating." Of course the aim is to win, and this is how we do it.

There is probably nothing we believe in more strongly than the importance of happiness in the workplace. It is absolutely the key to providing superior service. Of course our clients are the reason for our existence as a company, but to serve our clients best we have to put our people first.

The principle behind it is straightforward. It's our people who provide service to our clients. The highest achievable level of service comes from the heart. So, the company that reaches its people's hearts will provide the very best service. It's the nicest thing we could possibly do for our *clients*. They have come to learn that by being second, they come out ahead.

It's kind of like the old story about the horse and the cart. Let's say our people represent the horses. If we put our clients in the cart and put them out front they aren't going to go very far. We can have champagne, caviar, and cable TV in that cart and our clients still aren't going anywhere as long as the horses are behind them.

We feel that way about our people. If we put our people first, they'll put our clients first. Sure, we have to do a lot of other things right too, but we contend that this is the aspect of service most often forgotten, and that's why it's the one I talk about most.

According to a theory of psychologist Abraham Maslow, human needs fall into a natural hierarchy from most to least pressing. These needs are related to physiology, safety, social acceptance, esteem, and self-actualization. People are driven to satisfy the most critical need and then will move on to the next most important.

If a person has food, clothing, shelter, security, companionship, and self-esteem, only then will he or she be motivated by self-improvement. While most companies provide for people's basic provisions, we contend that it's essential to create an environment in which higher-level needs are satisfied.

If people are concerned about job security, internal politics, or other typical workplace frustrations, they're not going to be concentrating on the customer. They'll be worrying about themselves. We try to create a climate in which our people leave those worries to the company so they can and will focus solely on our clients.

Companies are only fooling themselves when they believe that "The Customer Comes First." People do not inherently put the customer first, and they certainly don't do it because their employer expects it. Only when people know what it feels like to be first in someone else's eyes can they sincerely share that feeling with others.

We're not saying choose your people over your customers. We're saying focus on your people *because* of your customers. That way everybody wins.

Setting the Tone
The Importance of Accessible Leadership

In the November 1991 issue of *Working Woman,* contributing editor and author Nancy Austin writes about Bill Arnold, president of Centennial Medical Center in Nashville: "One of his first acts at Centennial was to shatter sacrosanct management tradition by yanking his office door from its hinges and suspending it from the lobby ceiling to underscore his commitment to an open-door policy."

People emulate those who lead them, so starting at the top and emanating throughout the organization, leaders must always be cognizant of the examples they set. In our company, the leadership approach is to be approachable.

We need contact at every level. It's the only way to avoid the purification of information as it filters its way up the organization. It's human nature to want to share only the good news with those who lead us and to try to fix problems quietly.

But we often learn more from our failures than we do from our successes. We need to know about problems that are being solved as well as those that are not. We can't ever look at time with our people as an interruption. It's the most important thing we do, and we can never do enough of it.

My Day Is Yours
A Program to Reach People

A couple of years ago I initiated a program in which anyone in the company could spend a day with me. Whatever my day includes, their day includes. They read what I read. They are a part of every phone call, client visit, meeting, or whatever else makes up my day. The only exception is any confidential human resource issue that might betray another associate's privacy.

We call this our "Associate of the Day" program, and at first it took place each Tuesday. But it was so well received that I began to host an Associate of the Day each Tuesday, Wednesday, and Thursday, and sometimes two associates per day. The tradition still continues each week, but now we've expanded it to all leadership positions. Associates can also spend a day with the vice president or director of their choice.

The program has been a tremendous success. Our associates learn more about the company, they get a good look at the overall picture of the company, and hopefully they return to their jobs with renewed enthusiasm for the importance of their part in our goals. They come away with a greater understanding of the level of responsibility their leaders carry.

On the other hand, the program has helped our leaders learn more about the needs, aspirations, and talents of our people. It has helped us to spot future leaders and earmark growth areas for them. It helps people chart their career paths as well. Someone may think they'd like a career in a particular department and after spending a day there they might decide it's not for them. They learn what a department really does before working toward becoming a part of it and possibly being disappointed later.

The program also forces us to take a good look at how we're spending our days. Quite honestly, when someone is watching you, it's embarrassing to have a slow moment, to procrastinate on a project or decision, or not to give your best every minute of the day.

Feeling Like a Sandwich
A Program to Reach Middle-Level Leaders

They say that often the middle child in a family feels somewhat forgotten. The eldest child benefits from the sense of excitement that parents feel over their new role. The baby of a family is often spoiled not just by the parents, but also by the child's brothers and sisters. But the middle child sometimes gets lost in the shuffle.

It seems to be the same with middle-level leaders— supervisors and managers. A great deal is expected of them. They're placed in the challenging position of communicating what comes from above to those on the front line and vice versa. They're caught in the middle.

It seems more and more companies are recognizing the benefits of supporting their frontline people. And we don't need to worry too much about those at the top, but what about the people in the middle?

In our company, the Associate of the Day program attracts mostly entry-level associates, and while the program is open to everyone, these are the people I most hoped would participate. On the other hand, I meet with our top leaders almost daily. So I needed a program to reach middle-level leaders.

I hold meetings at least eight times a week with mid-level managers throughout the company. During these meetings, I ask for their evaluation of the morale and effectiveness of their departments and for their suggestions for improvements. We discuss their personal career goals and anything else that's on their minds.

If a common barrier for middle management is a lack of big-picture perspective, I claim upper management just as often lacks understanding of the microworkings of their organizations. Through this program, I've gained a greater understanding of each department's area of expertise, such as telecommunications, accounting, or technology. These "departmental reports" have also taught me more about what's really happening in the company. They've broadened my perspective by removing one more layer in the information filtering process.

Happiness Barometer
A Way to Measure Happiness

The only way we can ever really know if we reach our goals is to try to measure our progress. The same goes with happiness in the workplace. We can't just assume our people are happy. We have to be sure they are, and that means finding ways to help them tell us.

About two years ago, we assembled a focus group of twenty people who are representative of our associate population. They come from a variety of offices, departments, lines of business, and geographic locations. Some have been with the company for a relatively short time and others for several years.

Twice a year I meet with this group for an entire day to get a read on the morale of our people. Each meeting begins with an anonymous questionnaire. It's the same one every time so we can monitor changes. While the questions are open-ended to solicit discussion, each contains a numerical rating so we can quantify morale and track its fluctuations.

The questions all have to do with happiness in the workplace. We ask the participants to evaluate things like their leadership, benefits, and work fulfillment. We ask them to voice their frustrations and make suggestions. They answer from personal experience, but they also tell us how those in their particular office, department, or line of business are feeling.

The rest of the meeting is left for open discussion. Already we have instituted two major changes as a result of this group's input: One was to start a 401k contribution program, and the other was to establish an internal department to help our associates plan their own personal travel.

Open Lines of Communication
Using Voice Mail to Encourage Feedback

Last year, we created a voice mail program for our associates. They can call any time, from anywhere, about anything. We review every message and get back to those requesting a response.

People can leave anonymous messages, but almost everyone seems to leave their name and number. We get a lot of questions, and that's good. For the most part, the calls fall into three categories: ideas, career considerations, and talk about morale.

People have called with suggestions ranging from offering hang gliding at our corporate retreat (explained in Chapter 14, "Blazing New Trails") to establishing an exchange program with the educational system in which teachers could work at our company for a year while specialists from technology or other departments would teach in the schools. One associate from our Chicago office suggested that we work with the Red Cross to provide CPR training to all associates. Another in Daytona Beach recommended that we videotape meetings that take place at headquarters and send the tapes out to the field offices.

Several of the suggestions were cost-saving ideas, like the one from an associate in our Lancaster, Pennsylvania, office who proposed a program to cut down on unnecessary postage. He calculated we could save up to $100,000 per year just by using plain white envelopes for internal purposes as opposed to our letterhead envelopes and by always using the smallest envelope possible. So far, his idea has saved the company more than $22,000.

We get a lot of calls from people expressing an interest in pursuing a particular career path within the company—most of them in sales. Along those same lines, we are inundated with calls suggesting certain accounts we should contact, asking the status of potential accounts, and offering assistance with the sales process.

We've also uncovered areas of concern through the voice mailbox program. On a couple of occasions we saw a pattern of several calls from the same office about a variety of concerns from staffing to local office policies. That told us we had some underlying leadership and communication issues to resolve there that had not surfaced prior to the calls.

Many of the calls requested more visits from senior leaders to our four hundred offices in the field. A clear majority of the calls regarded a hiring and pay increase freeze in effect for several months in 1991: About a third were to suggest ways to ease us through it; another third were to protest it; and the final third were to say thanks for not laying anyone off.

There's nothing radical about voice mail. What's helpful is that something so simple could be so powerful when applied to making people's lives better. It's a way to make it as easy as possible for people to tell us what's important to them.

Business or Life-Style?
Earning the Right to Be Part of Our People's Lives

Most of our waking hours are spent at work. Therefore, employers have a tremendous effect on the personal as well as business lives of their people—in fact, too much of an effect. As much as we all try, it's next to impossible to truly "leave work at work" and become a new person at home.

When something at work is on our minds, we aren't able to enjoy the little time we have at home. Then, the following day, we feel bad while at work for not having spent enough "quality" time with our family. We're concerned while at home over our lack of productivity during the day. The cycle repeats itself over and over again and people spiral downward.

This is no way to succeed either at home or at work, and it's no way to live. For that reason, our company ranks happiness in the workplace among our highest priorities. And I have made it my personal crusade.

Companies should strive to be as much life-styles as businesses but they have to earn that right. They need to pay more attention to the humanistic side of business. It's said that it's not a good idea to work with friends. Hogwash. Friends don't let each other down. Who will people go that extra mile for—a friend or a detached business colleague?

To get people to "live" a company, it needs to more closely resemble life. Typical corporate structure is alien to the way people interact with one another naturally. We try to avoid the typical structure, which is often pretentious and isolating.

For example, we don't have layers upon layers of management and we don't have a large support staff. We strive to do most of our own communicating. To look at an organizational chart for our company you'd need an awfully wide piece of paper. We try to make our structure as flat as possible.

I have eleven people reporting directly to me, and they each have several direct reports, and so on. That way communication flows more freely both ways and we all open ourselves to closer contact with a greater number of people. This feeds creativity and makes our decisions more well rounded on every level.

What Have You Done for Them Lately?
People Are the One True Competitive Measure

The happiness of life is made up of minute fractions— the little soon forgotten charities of a kiss or smile, a kind look, a heartfelt compliment, and the countless infinitesimals of pleasurable and genial feeling.

—Samuel Taylor Coleridge,
"The Friend. The Improvisatore"

The big things in life certainly matter, but the little things can really add up. They can build happiness, commitment, and well-being, or they can chip away at a person's self-esteem, security, and outlook.

So far, I've discussed the bigger issues—the foundation of putting our people first, programs to ensure accessibility of leadership, creative ways to measure happiness. But I haven't talked about the little day-to-day things that help contribute to fulfillment among our people.

Even something as basic as celebrating each person's birthday, anniversary with the company, or other special occasion should be considered important business. My co-author tells me that in a company where she worked previously, such occasions were celebrated for years until a new company head banned such activity during the workday, and morale took a nosedive.

As hokey as it may sound, we have "jeans days" which disprove the "dress for success" theory. We're every bit as productive on those days, if not more. There are also days when people dress like their account, wearing clothing that has the company's logo or keeping its products on their desk. Or sometimes, people wear costumes that reflect their favorite destination in a contest to win a trip there.

Our company offers "familiarization" trips for both educational and enjoyment purposes. This gives people the opportunity to learn more about the destinations where we send our clients, while traveling together and getting to know each other better.

We give our people one to three weeks (depending on their tenure) paid time to participate, and we give them $100 to $400 (again, depending on length of time with the company) toward the trips, many of which are free to begin with. This is in addition to vacation time.

An activities committee sets up exchange programs between offices, departments, and positions. They organize lunches where everyone brings a different salad ingredient, creating a giant salad bar. Or sometimes offices will gather for lunch, rent a movie, and eat popcorn.

Most offices keep a scrapbook with photos of these activities, letters of compliment to associates, and other mementos of shared experiences. These are all activities that foster happiness and encourage teamwork. Each office plans whatever they like. The important point is that they are not just permitted—they are invited—to do so.

I believe companies earn the bad attitudes of their people. Does anyone ever begin a new job with a bad attitude? No. They are "bright-eyed and bushy-tailed," filled with anticipation, excitement, and ambition. But companies with little regard for the happiness of their people find that their enthusiasm and open-mindedness are soon replaced by apathy and bitterness.

I was once discussing the concept of happiness in the workplace with the CEO of a company during a luncheon. We agreed that it's vital to a healthy work force and to providing good service. But we disagreed on one important point—that it's the company's responsibility to ensure the happiness of its people. When I told him some of the things we do to encourage happiness he said, "If they're not happy in our company, we fire them." I didn't take him literally, but at the same time, his message was clearly that companies shouldn't coddle their people.

Cries from corporate America lament a lack of motivation in the workplace, absenteeism, turnover, apathy, lethargy, and a host of other evils that drag down productivity in our country and make us a less fierce global competitor. The origin of these maladies is a lack of happiness in the workplace. Without it, the best-planned processes, the finest tools, and most marketable products go to waste. Without it, eventually all else breaks down.

Every year we hold a dinner for our clients at which the keynote speaker is the CEO of a major industry force. I remember a conversation I had with one keynote speaker just prior to his remarks. He had just been appointed chief executive of a prominent airline. He asked me what I would suggest, as his client and partner, to turn the somewhat troubled carrier around.

I told him I certainly wasn't an expert in running an

airline, but I do try to understand people and what motivates them, makes them happy, helps them to provide outstanding service. My only suggestion to him was to put his desk on an airplane.

I told him if I were running his company, I'd make my office a different flight each day, and my time would be spent talking with my people and the clients on board. I never asked him if he did it or not, but I do know that his airline has come back strong and its service is among the best.

If more corporations paid as much attention to their people as they do to politics, public image, and increased profits, everything else would fall into place. Profits are a natural extension of happiness in the workplace. It doesn't work the other way around. We are consistently able to trace higher costs to cases of unhappiness in specific departments and offices. We take it very seriously.

Uprooting Unhappiness
The Story of a Costly Mistake

As important as happiness in the workplace is to us, we have certainly made mistakes. That's why it's so important never to waiver from our pursuit of it.

A couple of years ago we acquired a major account that warranted the opening of a new office. Our new client was anxious to have us begin service and asked that we start earlier than we planned. We didn't want to disappoint them so we rushed ahead.

We made a lot of mistakes by not following our normal process. We hired a leader for the office based on recommendation. We didn't employ our practice of placing potential leaders in uncomfortable situations and interviewing them under a variety of circumstances (explained in Chapter 5, "Finding the Right People"). We hired all of our new people for that office too quickly.

The first sign that things were wrong was our error rate there. We've learned that's almost always a sign of unhappiness. The second sign was that our people in that location began to call my office to tell me they were unhappy. The third sign was when our client called to tell me that the company's travelers weren't pleased with the service in our new office.

What's interesting is that the client was the last to feel the effects of our people's unhappiness. There's a tremendous opportunity here. Unhappiness surfaces before client dissatisfaction. So by paying attention to our people, we can turn the tide before problems affect service. The best way to do it is to concentrate on building in happiness, up front.

To turn the situation around, a team of human resources associates set up shop in that office, talking with people, trying to get to the root of the problems. They went for a day and stayed more than a month. What they found was "old style" leadership: the treatment of people as a means to an end. We worked with our leaders there, but most of them just didn't fit, culturally. Only those with the human instinct were retained.

We met with our associates in small groups and asked which leaders were instilling fear and which cared more about their own advancement than their people. We asked them who neglected to make time for them and who was unfair. I went to that office several times to sit down and talk with our people. Those were some of the worst days in my career. I could see the negative effects our company was having on their lives. We had made the classic mistakes that so many others make.

We had to start over, to show our people the company was there for them, before we could ever expect them to feel they were truly there for our clients. And when we did, service improved drastically. Our clients are delighted with their service in that office, but it cost us a great deal to get there.

During this period, there were twenty-seven turn-overs—people whom we had trained at a cost of $61,290—and that was money out the door. To replace those people, we spent an additional $50,000 in recruiting costs (advertisements and search firms). These are just hard costs. More was lost in terms of time and perception.

Three human resource managers devoted what ended up being a quarter of the year to solving the problems created in this one office, so that adds up to 75 percent of a single person-year exhausted on the effort. In addition to the time, there were three legal complaints. We were successful in all of them, and while there was no cost in payments of any kind, they took time and energy, and morale took a beating.

But in addition to lost productivity there were negative effects on our service to our clients in that city, and shaken confidence on the part of our associates. These hurt most of all.

A company is only as good as its people. We can all buy the same machines and tools, but it's people who apply them creatively. We can hire consultants for direction, but when it all comes down to it, their advice is only as valuable as the people who will implement their suggestions. Our true competitive measure is our people.

Pillars of People
Building a Foundation for Happiness

Every company operates on a hierarchy of concerns. Ours is: people, service, profits. In that order. The company's focus is on its people. Our people then focus on serving our clients. Profits are the end result.

The pillars upon which many companies are built are primarily profit-oriented. We contend these pillars are not strong enough to hold the weight of companies, particularly in lean times. Human beings must be the pillars of a company. They provide an unshakable foundation. This might appear to be a soft strategy but, in our case, we rely on our growth and client retention rates to prove that this method translates into solid results.

Cultivating Happiness in the Workplace
A Summary

- Happiness in the workplace is key to providing superior service. Continually create an environment where your people leave the worrying to the company so they can focus on your clients.

- People are companies' one true competitive measure. Take a look at areas with rising costs to see if there's a correlating morale problem.

- Measuring happiness in the workplace is essential. Four ways we have found effective are: (1) asking people to draw what the company means to them; (2) meeting with middle-level managers to get a read on morale within specific departments; (3) using voice mail to encourage feedback; (4) assembling a focus group to regularly test morale.

- Make contact with your people at every level. Fight the purification of information as it rises to meet you. You will learn more about what's really happening in your company and morale will soar. Consider an "Associate of the Day" program. Leaders learn as much from it as their people do.

- Make your company a life-style—not just a place to work. Make it fun. Be ever cognizant of the effect your company has on your people's personal as well as professional lives. Remember always to involve your people in decisions; give them a sense of ownership in your company.

- Recheck the ratio of financial to humanistic pillars in your company's foundation. We have found that the two coexist in perfect harmony. The humanistic approach to business yields the financial results companies seek because people work better when they *want* to work.

CHAPTER 4

INVENTING THE FUTURE

There's a kid in every neighborhood who's always in charge. In mine, it was Billy. Whatever he said was final. He invented the rules of the game so it's no wonder he always won. He was small but fast, so when we played football it was always touch football, not tackle. And he was always either the quarterback or the receiver. He made sure he'd be the one to score.

He happened to be ambidextrous, so when we played dodgeball, he would suggest that everyone play with the hand they didn't favor. He always placed himself at an advantage. People seldom questioned why. Everyone wanted desperately to be like him and he knew it. He made sure it was that way.

I've never forgotten the power people hold when they invent the rules of the game. For that reason we strive, as a company, to continually invent the future of our industry. That way we secure a prominent place in it for ourselves and our clients.

To illustrate some of the ways in which a company can

41

redefine itself, I'll identify five pivotal decisions that were instrumental in taking us from a local company to a national company, to the global firm we're becoming today. Our ventures into uncharted waters have told us that it's worth the uncertain journey.

First—Taking Deregulation by the Horns
Turning Change into Opportunity

The changes brought upon our industry by deregulation of the airlines were seen by many, if not most, travel agencies as a closed door. Agencies saw the uncertainty of their future role as a death sentence for their companies, and for many it was. But we looked at deregulation as the opportunity of a lifetime.

We knew that from that point on, we'd no longer be limited to the role of reservation taker and ticket deliverer. We were about to enter the business of information management. Open skies meant "all's fair," which in turn meant rapid changes in schedules and airfares. We knew people were going to need a lot of help. We said, "Bring on the commotion!" Then we positioned ourselves as the solution.

A small group of us used to work late and then go to a place called "The Top of the Two's." Believe it or not, we'd sit and talk about how exciting the new world of travel would be. Over a few beers, we'd map out our dreams for the future. From our viewpoint, the change in regulation made room for a higher level of service. We took deregulation by the horns and delivered it to our clients in the form of solid advantage.

This was the point at which we realized that corporate travel would be affected the most by deregulation. Now companies had opportunities for savings that didn't exist before. Prior to deregulation, the airfare choices between cities were basically limited to first class and coach. Suddenly there were new routes, new carriers, and almost daily, new fares. There were so many choices for business travelers in this new climate, and we made it our job to find the best ones for our clients.

We ran out and got computers for everyone in our corporate travel department and set out to make sense of the chaos. We did our research and we showed companies that travel was now a controllable expense (which we were prepared to manage for them). They took us up on our offer, and our corporate travel business boomed.

Prior to deregulation, corporate travel represented less than a quarter of our business. Today it's well over 90 percent. Because we weren't afraid of change, but on the contrary hungered for it, we seized an opportunity to completely redefine our business.

Changes in regulations, a competitor's new product launch—any restyling that takes place around you holds promise for you to capitalize on it. Sometimes even changes we dread can be the best thing for us. They force us to face the future.

Second—Strength in Numbers
Reshaping for Growth

Demand for our services in corporate travel management grew and we expected that growth would explode. We banked on that projection, and in 1981 we opened the travel agency industry's first reservation center and hired over one hundred people to take corporate reservations.

This was a big investment for us. It called for significant human and capital resources. A lot of people in our industry thought we were strapping ourselves with a "white elephant." We were convinced otherwise.

We invested in advanced technology that would enable us to capture data on the travel patterns of our corporate clients. We used that information collectively to negotiate with the airlines on our clients' behalf.

While we were gathering and analyzing these statistics, a lot of other agencies were letting it slip past them, in the wake of the storm caused by deregulation. Having a central system to capture this information was critical, and it gave us a sustainable competitive advantage.

The reservation center enabled us to share expertise, information, and resources to serve our clients better. At the same time, we were preparing for future growth. Today, we have reservation centers across the country, one in London, and a joint venture in Japan.

Planning the structure for rapid growth proved to be a self-fulfilling prophecy for us. Just as most architectural plans include potential extensions, growth plans help a company to prepare for expansion and they also can *provide* the opportunity for growth, because it's comforting to potential clients to know a company is ready to handle their business.

Third—Go Big or Go Home
Growth Without Gambling

By 1984, we were by far the strongest regional player in corporate travel management, but then something happened that pushed us over the edge to national status. The Du Pont Company awarded Rosenbluth its national travel account. At that time, it was the single largest corporate travel management program in history.

Taking on this account meant we had to go national. This is something we had wanted to do, but we decided it was too risky to speculate in new markets without national recognition. Being awarded this account allowed us to grow into all of Du Pont's major markets because we had the business to warrant it. From there, we acquired new accounts in each of those locations.

Our partnership with Du Pont has saved them over $150 million, so it's not surprising that it set off an industry trend for corporations to consolidate their travel accounts on a nationwide basis. And we were positioned as the leader in consolidation. We began to share our expertise and resources with corporation after corporation, consolidating their travel programs. We continued to grow with our clients, entering their major markets. Then we attracted additional business in each of those cities.

Our client-driven approach to growth ensures that our focus remains on our clients, but at the same time, it ensures our expansion. Because every new location exists to serve a client, we take minimal risk in our investment of capital and human resources. This guarantees that we'll be around to serve the clients for whom we've expanded. So as you can see, at times being conservative or risk-adverse is, in fact, defining the future.

Critical mass can be important for a company, and achieving it presents its share of hurdles. But we've found that the client-driven approach to growth not only makes better business sense, it usually means better client service.

Fourth—Complete Independence
Breaking Ties That Constrain You

The best relationships are on an even scale. Both partners bring value to the table and have the freedom to maintain their own identity. This seems to be especially true in a company like ours—headstrong and a little unusual.

Our company works best in an environment of complete independence, where our creativity and willingness to take calculated risks are not hampered. As we continued to grow, we quickly discovered we needed to claim independence in our back-room technology in order to serve our clients better than anyone else.

Most companies have some form of front-room and back-room systems. In our industry, travel agencies usually depend on an airline for their systems. The front-room system provides flight schedules, airfares, and entry into the reservations process. The back-room system provides accounting, data base, and programming capabilities.

In the front room we declared our independence when we created READOUT®, proprietary software that fuses airfare data from all the major airlines into one system (explained in Chapter 7, "Technology as a Tool"). We had all the schedule and pricing information we needed right at our fingertips.

But in the back room, where data is stored and analyzed, independence was another story—and still is, for most agencies. Common practice is to utilize a back-room system originating from an airline. But we had to have our own. (This system too is explained more fully in Chapter 7.)

Creating our own back-room system was one of the most expensive and most important decisions we ever made. Why was it so expensive?

Because these multimillion-dollar back-room systems are subsidized by the airlines for agencies that utilize them. They're either provided for free or leased at a greatly reduced price. Breaking away from this arrangement meant we would have to build our own system and bear all the costs.

Why was this so important? For the very same reason that it was so expensive: The airline subsidy meant dependence upon the airline with which you subscribed, and a certain distance from those with which you didn't subscribe.

We decided that information was the key to effectively and proactively managing our clients' travel programs. We'd only take control of that information and be free to use it to benefit our clients if we built our own back-room system. The following hypothetical example illustrates the value of that independence.

Suppose that a travel agency subscribes to airline ABC's back-room system. A key client has a high volume of travel between two particular cities, and could fly either airline ABC or airline XYZ on that route. The client and the agency decide it would be more advantageous to consolidate that traffic with one airline, with which they can negotiate the strongest arrangement for price discounts and service enhancements. The agency's dependence upon airline ABC's back-room system presents some complications.

Complication #1: In order to bring strength to the bargaining table, the agency and client must have their complete travel history between those routes. In order to do so, they have to ask airline ABC for that data. The purpose for it would be clear to the airline. Why would they want to provide that information when they perceive it as being used against them in negotiations?

Complication #2: If they do retrieve the data and airline XYZ makes a better offer than airline ABC, can the agency ask airline ABC to write a program to redirect market share to airline XYZ in order to take advantage of the better offer?

Sure, they can ask, but do you think that airline ABC will put a project high on its priority list that steers business *away* from its own company? Of course not.

When you get your ammunition from the person with whom you're negotiating, you're not in a position of strength. While the airlines are our partners in creating the most highly effective travel management programs for our clients, the negotiating balance is skewed by dependence upon them.

Through independence and three-way partnerships, we can ensure a win-win-win outcome for our clients, our suppliers, and our company. Our clients lower their travel costs, our airline partners fill more seats, and we can market our ability to provide these savings to potential clients.

A careful look at levels of dependence upon outside sources is wise. Though partnerships can multiply our capabilities, a level of dependence that holds us back from serving our clients to the best of our ability is dangerous. Independence can be achieved without harm to our partnerships.

Fifth—Spanning the Globe
Global Expansion Through Strategic Alliances

In his farewell address on September 17, 1796, George Washington said, " 'Tis our true policy to steer clear of permanent alliances, with any portion of the foreign world." Back then when the world seemed vast and the country was just starting out that might have been a reasonable policy, but in today's global climate those words show how times have changed.

While a global presence is becoming increasingly more important for companies, it's not easy to achieve. For many companies, the leap across the Atlantic or Pacific is out of reach. There was a time when it seemed that was true for us as well, but there are creative ways to make that leap.

It was our track record in managing nationally consolidated travel programs that led to the next logical step for expansion—global. Here too, our approach was and is client-driven. Several years ago, our multinational clients began to ask us if we could serve them around the world, so we set out to find the best way.

We studied the feasibility of opening international offices and compared that with the practicality of learning each individual market from an expert there, and decided the latter was a better approach. At the time, opening our own offices overseas would not have been a good use of capital, and we recognized that we didn't have the leadership in place to properly manage it. This turned out to be a very wise decision for us.

We developed the Rosenbluth International Alliance (RIA), which is designed to be flexible enough to take advantage of business opportunities that arise in any part of the world at any time. After extensive research, we formed alliances with what we considered to be the very best travel management firm in each of over forty countries around the world. What we looked for was a match in philosophy and values, dedication to service, an orientation toward technology, and financial stability.

We benefit from the strong position each member holds in its marketplace, and from its knowledge of the local culture, government regulations, suppliers, and business climate. So we're able to concentrate on service.

The key to the Alliance is our ability to globally collect

travel information for our multinational clients while delivering the best service on a local basis. In a few select markets, we have elected to open our own offices, make an acquisition, or establish joint ventures. The beauty of the program is that it is entirely flexible, and with the global changes that are taking place from day to day, that's essential.

From local to regional to national to global, and in the future, maybe beyond global, growth is a matter not just of a company's size, but of its service. There are numerous steps in providing outstanding service: finding the right people to provide it, arming them with the training and technology to do their best, and of course, having a service orientation that speaks your company's language. I'll cover them all in the coming chapters.

Critical Decisions
A *Summary*

- Look for opportunities that surround change—in your industry, in legislation, even in your competitors' strategy. Airline deregulation created a world of opportunity for our company.

- Develop a growth plan. It not only ensures you'll be ready for expansion, but it may even give you the chance to grow, because clients feel comfortable knowing you're ready to serve them. Our plan supports our client-driven approach to growth.

- Take a careful look at your levels of dependence upon outside sources. Partnerships are great, but not if they get in the way of serving your clients to their best advantage.

CHAPTER 5

FINDING THE RIGHT PEOPLE

Most of us choose our spouse with care and rear our children with nurturing and compassionate attention. Yet we tend to select the people who will join our company on the basis of an interview or two, and once they have joined, they often find they must fend for themselves.

This contrast illustrates the disparity between the family and work environments. But given the amount of time we must spend at work, wouldn't we all be happier if we took as much care at the office as at home to create a supportive environment? Wouldn't we also be far more successful? I say yes, and yes again.

Service Begins in the Heart
The Importance of Looking for Nice People

Tenet number one is *Look for nice people*. The rest will fall into place. Too often, a person's job history carries

more weight than his or her human values. What's in someone's heart can't be discovered in a résumé.

There's the type of person who pushes his way to the
front of the line to snare a seat on the commuter train and
the type of person who offers his seat to others. There are
people whose favorite line is "That's not my job," and those
who are quick to ask how they can help.

Some people can't wait until others finish their sen-
tences so they can talk about themselves or their viewpoints. But there are those who really want to listen to
what others have to say. Some look to gain; others seek to
contribute.

In our selection process, kindness, caring, compassion,
and unselfishness carry more weight than years on the job,
an impressive salary history, and stacks of degrees.

It's something our competition always seems to try to
figure out. At its most basic common denominator, the
formula for our company's success is that we have more
nice people than they do. Niceness is among our highest
priorities because nice people do better work.

Our clients time and again tell us that they see our
people as an oasis in the corporate desert. They actually
look forward to talking with our people. This is no accident.
We take pains to ensure it. There's no greater competitive
advantage in a service business.

You can't teach people to be nice. You can't just say,
"Thursday, begin caring!" Caring must be inherent in their
natures—they have to feel it in their hearts. And if they
do, their clients will feel it too.

One of my proudest moments came during an interview
with a prospective associate who was considering relocating
to Philadelphia from the Midwest to work for Rosenbluth.
Coming to the city for her third interview, she arrived at

the airport and hailed a taxi. When the driver asked her where she wanted to go, she replied, "Rosenbluth Travel, at Nineteenth and Arch streets." His response to her request will remain with me forever. He said, "Rosenbluth Travel. Now that's where all the nice people work." After hearing that, our interviewee wanted very much to become a part of our company, and she subsequently did. In fact, she's the coauthor of this book.

This particular reputation is more rewarding than any other we could earn and, in my mind, that justifies our ultrastringent criteria for joining the company. Each person selected must act as an ambassador for us and must be chosen accordingly.

It's important to remember that no matter how impressive people's résumés or previous accomplishments are, if they're not nice and don't fit they can't be right. Why run the risk of contaminating the team?

Only the Best
You Can't Afford Not to Be Picky

We take a selective posture toward inviting people into our company. For each position, we interview eight to ten people before making our final selection. And the interviewing isn't easy—why should it be? We expect a great deal from our people and offer them a lot in return. We owe it to each other to select only people who will enrich what we have built.

Just as a money manager analyzes an individual stock by considering how it will fit into his portfolio, companies must evaluate prospective employees with this same unblinking eye. An individual stock, although possibly a good performer on its own, might have negative effects on the overall portfolio.

Likewise, individuals should be selected for what they bring to the team as much as for their personal potential. A key component to team fit is cultural fit. In order to make the right decision, companies must be able to get their arms around their culture and envision prospective employees within it. There's no place this is more important than in the area of leadership, because leaders will be looked upon as role models for people throughout your company.

Big Dogs, Tall Weeds
Selecting Senior Leaders

It's often been said, "If you want to run with the big dogs, you have to learn to deal with the tall weeds." Interviewing top leaders is a special process for us, because our leaders are a breed all their own. Candidates go through some pretty strange and stringent evaluations.

By the time leaders enter this company, we know what they eat for breakfast, when they lose their temper, and exactly where they will fit in. We've found that getting to know someone that well can only be achieved by observing them in incongruous scenarios that have nothing to do with the position, the company, or business at all.

Behind the Wheel or Under the Hoop
Unusual Interviewing Techniques

Take driving habits, for example. We think they say a lot about people. We don't want to hire the type of person who can't drive decisively or who doesn't look for alternatives to traffic jams, just accepting their fate of being at a standstill. On the other hand, we don't want someone who is reckless or distracted. We don't want anyone who puts "getting there" before the safety of his passengers. These are all traits that can be carried into the workplace.

Another acid test is sports. We like competitive people who are driven to do their best. But equally important are the ability and desire to work for the good of the team. Each player needs to possess that innate selflessness that comes from being secure enough not to need to be the star every moment of the game. We value the person who is eager to pass the ball to the open player as much as we value the superstar who can slam-dunk like Michael Jordan.

We were once saved by a softball game. In the final stages of our search for a key senior leader, we invited a top candidate to join our leaders in a game of softball. His true colors really showed during that outing. He had to be the star, even at the expense of others. His team lost and he took it poorly, looking to place the blame on his teammates.

We asked him to play softball because we weren't positive about him, but we never expected to learn so much. These were traits that went all but undetected during his interviews. Smooth operators *can* slip through the cracks, but when they are evaluated in nontraditional ways, they reveal much more about themselves.

It's important to get as many people as possible involved in the selection process, because we need to bring into the company only those who can work well with the team we have in place. For that reason, candidates for senior leadership positions spend time with our current senior leaders, and their input is crucial. To round out the process, prospective leaders are often interviewed by those they will lead as well. We're seeking people who will inspire their teams. Who better to make that judgment than the team itself?

Put to the Test
Employing Executive Assessments

Because finding our company's top leaders is handled like microsurgery, several years ago we began an executive assessment program to evaluate candidates for senior positions. These evaluations are conducted by a corporate psychologist and the team of leaders of which the candidate seeks to be a member.

Those new to the company as well as current associates being considered for promotion into senior leadership positions must participate. The assessments analyze values, personality traits, and strengths and weaknesses, as well as determining team fit. Each leader is unique, but it's crucial that as a group they complement one another's strengths and shore up one another's weakneses. Most important, they have to enjoy working together as a team.

Because our assessments are conducted, in part, by a corporate psychologist, his understanding of our company's goals is key to the effectiveness of the program. For that reason, he is often included in our strategic planning sessions and other key meetings, though he is not employed by our company. We do, however, retain him to be available to help our people manage difficult situations either at work or in their private lives. We think it's a sound investment in our people, and have assumed the costs of even entirely personal consultations.

The Right Stuff
There Are Tools to Help You

Have you ever gone shopping, and after trying on what seems like a million things, bought something without trying it on? It's usually no surprise that when you finally try it on at home, it doesn't fit. Or how about the time you ordered something from a catalog that looked great in the picture, but when it arrived you were embarrassed to have ordered it? Then there's the day after Christmas. It's the biggest shopping day of the year—not because everything's on sale but because we're all returning gifts that don't fit or that we don't like, or maybe we don't even know what they are.

The same bad fit happens with people and companies, but people aren't so easy to return. There are a lot of folks out there and they're not all going to fit in your company.

The recruiting and selection process is labor-intensive and expensive. Hiring mistakes take emotional as well as financial tolls. Every company wants to find the right people the first time around.

Experts can be helpful in establishing criteria for good fit between employment candidates and your company, even its specific departments and positions. Several years ago, our human resources staff consulted a corporate psychologist to work with them to create a selection process for new associates that helps identify the best people for our company. Part of that process includes specially designed profiles of the appropriate personality type and repertoire of skills needed for specific positions within the company.

For example, the position of corporate travel reservationist calls for someone who will work with our clients on a day-to-day basis via telephone. A combination of technical, interpersonal, and organizational skills is required.

Our profile creation process was quite scientific, and had several steps. First, we put together a study group representative of our reservationist population. Next, we created a job analysis to define the position as it was on a day-to-day basis and to determine performance ideals. We identified key skills and characteristics that were fundamental to the position.

Then we applied tests in these areas to the group, such as reading and clerical efficiency, math reasoning, verbal fluency, and perception. Personality traits were also evaluated, such as energy, flexibility, rapport, assertiveness, and team contribution.

We compared the test scores of each person in the group with his or her performance on the job, to look for correlations between certain skills, personality traits, and success in the position. From these, we were able to derive prediction formulas which we can use to help us evaluate candidates during the selection process. These formulas are a way to determine likelihood of success in a particular capacity.

A certain degree of science removes some of the inherent subjectivity from the interviewing process. The profiles help us spot those people with the qualities that are likely to make them good candidates for a position and also more likely to enjoy their work, qualities that are mutually reinforcing.

While they are helpful as guidelines, profiles are not the sole criteria by which we select associates. We certainly don't want all of our people to be the same. But considering the fact that our company employs over one thousand reservationists, this process helps ensure that we achieve our standards and provide consistent service.

Similar profiles can be created for virtually any position in any industry, either through scientific studies like the one we employed, or simply through information gained from focus groups, performance appraisals, exit interviews, and other programs most likely in place. Perhaps a less formalized adaptation of the process could be helpful for companies not prepared to launch a full-scale program. Developing profiles for recurrent positions, however it's done, can save time and recruiting costs.

We learned something interesting from the study. The correlation between excellence in tasks and people skills was incredibly high. One explanation is that when people have the tasks down pat, they're free to concentrate on people skills. We also believe that nice people with a positive attitude instinctively master tasks so they can provide a level of service that supports their people skills.

The point is that the data from this study support our belief that nice people do a better job. Those who get along best with their colleagues and clients also have the best skills. By seeking nice people, you'll benefit your clients in both the tangible and intangible aspects of service.

Free from the Millstone of Ethnocentricity
The Benefits of Varied Backgrounds

People from a wide variety of backgrounds build depth into an organization. They offer a source of fresh ideas, new perspectives, and original applications for products, services, and resources. Because we commit extensive resources to our training programs we are not limited to looking only within our industry for quality people. This opens up new worlds for us in finding the best people.

Certainly, we hire experienced travel professionals, but more often we hire those who have excelled in their individual fields elsewhere. Rather than look for specialists in travel technology, for example, we seek technology experts from a variety of fields who will bring with them unique insight from other industries that may help change the future of ours.

Typically, our associates not only come from a wide variety of industries, but for the most part their experience is completely unrelated to travel. This broadens our horizons. These people offer perspectives that transcend our industry and give us a more vast understanding outside our sphere.

It all makes sense when you analyze it. For example, one of our automation specialists, who explains our technology products to our clients, came to our company from a career in special education. She has a gift of being able to explain complex concepts in understandable terms. She makes what could be a dry subject interesting. And she's an excellent listener.

Our director of industry relations is a Fulbright scholar and Vietnam veteran who, after working in the Peace Corps, taught high school history. His diplomatic skills are sharp, which is helpful in his negotiating work. His ability to instruct helps him clearly communicate our goals to our suppliers.

The variety of backgrounds is endless. One of our support agents is a retired postal worker. A primary part of this position is delivering tickets to our clients. It's a perfect fit.

A member of our human resources team is an electrical

engineer. She's charged with creating and updating human resource organizational systems. Her technical skills are being put to work in a creative application.

Our director of training is a former high school teacher and guidance counselor. He's obviously skilled in creating and presenting educational material. But he's also excellent at coaching people and evaluting their developmental needs, because of his work as a guidance counselor.

One of our account managers holds an MBA in international finance. Working closely with a corporate client to manage a multimillion-dollar travel account requires solid financial skills.

How do we find this vast array of people from such diverse backgrounds? Above all, we open ourselves to these possibilities by considering not *just* those whose résumés seem to fit the position. We take a great deal of care to interview a wide variety of people and to view their backgrounds with a creative eye. This is absolutely a competitive advantage.

Political Animals, Egotists, and Other Parasites
Personality Types to Avoid

We work to avoid contamination of our environment because it's not fair to the people we employ to have to work alongside those who aren't nice or who don't work hard. Our environment makes this company special, and we need to protect it to keep it that way.

There are three basic personality types we can spot a mile away, and we try never to allow them into our company. They are political animals, egotists, and freeloaders. They are often attracted to an organization like ours because they see the openness in our culture as rich hunting grounds for their own pursuits. Open, yes; naïve, no.

Political animals. The quickest way out of our company is to try to get ahead at the expense of others. This is covered in detail in Chapter 11, "The Gardening Process." But I want to state here and now that I believe politics and a successful organization are mutually exclusive.

Egotists. There's a fitting proverb that sums up egotism: "Those who say don't know and those who know don't say." Egotists seldom have a clear view of things. They're blinded by looking at every situation only to find the benefit to themselves. Their talents are foiled by poor judgment, and they destroy teamwork.

Confidence is fantastic but egotism is deadly. We'll take nice people with street smarts over arrogant "intellectuals" (who think they know it all) any day.

Freeloaders. Finally, there's the freeloader, otherwise known as the "travel hog" in our industry. Every industry has its own breed. They're along for a free piece of the product.

The term "travel agent" conjures up for many in the travel industry the image of a shrimp-scarfing nonprofessional, carousing through trade shows in search of free travel. Obviously this is a stereotype, but it's one we carefully avoid.

We're into minimal schmooze and maximum professionalism. Certainly, we provide excellent travel benefits to our people, and if they weren't interested in travel to a certain degree, they probably would not be drawn to a career in it. But free travel has to be so far down their list of priorities that it's almost an afterthought. This can be ascertained through a thorough interview process.

It begins from the very first contact we have with a

person, not just from the formal interview process itself. You can learn a great deal about a person through correspondence, phone calls, and casual interactions. Consistency is a good indicator of sincerity.

We're always on the lookout for nurturers and those who are mentally flexible. People who naturally and genuinely want to take care of others are ideal for service businesses, especially our company. Care givers also make for strong team players.

Mental flexibility is critical in a dynamic environment, and in today's lean organization, people need to be increasingly adaptable because fewer people are accomplishing more things. At our company, most of us think we know how we'll be spending our day, but it never fails to change. In fact, it's not unusual for our people to find themselves in a different city. People have to adapt quickly.

Those who are ruffled by a change in routine won't be happy here, so we try to determine that during the selection process. We might ask people about a typical day in their life or on the job. We ask them what they find frustrating. Or we create hypothetical situations (most based upon a real-life day around here) calling for flexibility, and we see how they react.

One of the best indicators is adaptability in the interview itself. We try to cut down on interruptions when interviewing, but there's bound to be at least one. The patience, good humor, and flexibility people display in their reactions to those interruptions say a lot.

The people we select must be professionals in every sense of the word, and they must want to build a career with us or they won't like it here. It's tough work and requires commitment to excellence and complete dedication to the company, fellow associates, and clients.

The Element of Danger
The Dangers of an Open Culture

Our unique culture has been the focus of quite a bit of attention, and this actually can leave a company vulnerable to those who are attracted to it with the wrong intentions.

We wear our culture on our sleeve, and people know what we're looking for. Sometimes the wrong person knows how to say and do just the right things. We've made some hiring mistakes because of this.

Since people tend to hire in their likeness, unhealthy pockets may form around them. There have been occasions when we've had to rebuild entire departments to turn such situations around.

If leaders listen carefully, their people will guide them to the problem. When we do find the cause, we try to give that person a second chance, and often it will work. But when they don't change swiftly and completely we have to ask ourselves if this one person has the right to have a negative effect on so many others. The answer is clearly "no."

The Annihilation of Arrogance
Tips for Conquering Pomposity

We believe strongly in the importance of combating arrogance. Trying to detect it during the selection process can help, but some is bound to slip in occasionally. Arrogance can even take root in those who normally are modest. The change comes about when turf is at stake or when they begin to feel they "own" a certain area.

Just to make sure we keep runaway egos in check, we regularly do teamwork exercises to illustrate the point that nobody has all of the answers. One of my favorites is "Green Vegetables," an exercise we learned years ago from a consultant.

In this exercise, people from all levels and all departments of the company write down all of the green vegetables they can recall in five minutes. Then each person reads his or her list out loud while someone from the group records all of the ideas.

Every time we hold this exercise the participants in the group are amazed at how many collective ideas were presented and how relatively few they could come up with on their own, compared to the group as a whole. The underlying message is one of synergy—not a new idea, but one that deserves continual emphasis. "The whole is greater than the sum of its parts." No individual's contributions will ever be as powerful on their own as they will be when strengthened by the contributions of the team.

Another ego-buster we rely upon is putting people in uncomfortable situations. People can often tell more about each other by spending an hour together with their guard down than they can by working together for a year.

One such experience for us was a "fence-building" project our top executives participated in during a strategic planning session. Our company holds these meetings twice a year, for our team of top leaders to strategize about the future and to strengthen the bonds among us.

During this particular meeting, our twelve top leaders and I set out to lay fence on a farm—not an everyday occurrence in corporate America. Suddenly, those who traditionally exude confidence—those to whom people come for answers—were wide-eyed and eager to tackle the new task that lay before them.

Everyone stood on equal ground, and to accomplish the job would require teamwork in the truest sense of the word. Interesting personality traits are revealed; heart and soul are bared when you manage to break down barriers and remove people from the environment they "own."

What happened surprised us all. Everyone was in charge. Everyone thought they knew how it should be done. We flew into action and the results were disastrous. The fence was finished in virtually no time, and it went in about as many directions as there were vice presidents. I think even the farm animals were laughing at us.

The farmer who owned the land was standing nearby. He possessed a wealth of knowledge about what we were trying to do. He had about twenty years of fence-laying experience under his belt. Tools that would have made the job much easier lay on the ground just a few yards away, untouched. They were unfamiliar to us, so they appeared to be of no value.

All chiefs and no Indians. All pride and not enough humility to seek guidance from those who could help. No process. No synergy. Poor quality. We learned some lessons that day that really made a difference.

Only after an hour of team humility did someone turn to the real expert, our farmer friend. Then, after two or three tries the fence stretched far beyond us around the perimeter of the pasture, and stood as a monument to the bonds we all knew were strengthened on that hot, dry day on a farm in North Dakota.

Formula for Finding the Right People
A Summary

- Choose wisely—the emotional and financial costs of turnover are high. Projects are put on hold, service is interrupted, training costs are lost, competitive information walks out the door, and a host of other ills result from turnover. You have to be sure you find the right people from the beginning. Look for team and cultural fit.

- When interviewing for leadership positions, place your candidates in situations beyond the normal scope of their work, or in environments away from the workplace—sports, driving, informal gatherings. Watch their interaction skills, see how they hold up in unexpected situations.

- Include as many people as possible in the interview process for key leaders. Those they will lead, as well as fellow key leaders, should have a say.

- You might consider utilizing the services of a corporate psychologist to help your company develop profiles for key positions or to help conduct executive assessments of potential senior leaders.

- Open your company up to a variety of backgrounds—not just from your own or related industries; not just the traditional sources for people. Broaden your horizons, widen your areas of expertise, and increase your chances for finding good people.

- Avoid arrogant people, egotists, political animals, and those who have their eye primarily on the benefits of your industry, such as free or discounted travel in the travel industry, cars in the auto industry, or whatever perks your particular industry offers.

- Exercises to keep egos in check can be helpful. They break down barriers, strengthen bonds, and help diminish turf wars. Situations that are slightly uncomfortable put a spotlight on people's true colors.

- Above all, look for nice people who care. Everything else can be taught.

CHAPTER 6

PERPETUAL TRAINING: A SECRET WEAPON

Leadership and learning are indispensable to each other.

—John Fitzgerald Kennedy, November 22, 1963

The growth of a company is really the aggregate of the growth of its individuals. Organizations that offer their people career-long training are investing in the future, while improving their firms today.

We made a decision in 1980 to become such a company. We've come a long way since that time. Today, our training goes far beyond the technical and extends outside our organization. It's been an interesting journey and one we've shared with a great many companies.

You might think, "Why would companies be interested in the training programs of a travel agency?" The answer is that much of our training is philosophical, attitudinal, and cultural. A number of client and nonclient firms have participated in our training programs.

The Kindergarten Principle
The Importance of Making Learning Enjoyable

Most kids really enjoy kindergarten. After that, they seem to enjoy the academic aspect of school progressively less each year. That's because a lot of the fun is taken out of learning as we get older.

It's a fact that people retain more when they learn through interaction. We've also proven that people retain a great deal more when they have fun learning. We call that "The Kindergarten Principle." We try to put the fun back in learning.

Why is it that kids who hate math can manage to learn the batting averages of just about every player in the American League? How come kids can learn to work with computers at such an early age and can beat almost any adult at Nintendo? They learn what they have fun learning.

Training is an attitude. For it to be effective, we must *want* to learn. Unfortunately, when we're required to learn something, we usually just memorize what we need to know. That's not learning.

True learning has become very important to this company. We consider it our responsibility to help each and every associate reach his or her full potential. If a hidden talent remains hidden and is not brought forth, nurtured, and developed, then we've failed as a company and as leaders.

We operate on the belief that there's nothing any of our associates couldn't learn if they wanted to. We try to select the type of person who thirsts for knowledge, and we keep rolling out new training programs to quench those thirsts.

Our clients depend on our people to be highly knowledgeable about every aspect of our service. They don't want people to be limited to understanding just the technical functions of their work. They want to interact with multifaceted individuals who can take care of whatever needs arise. This is never going to happen by accident.

Broad-based training prepares people to provide this level of service. Too many companies are anxious to get their new hires working. They thrust them into their new positions without adequate training. I contend that this is a mistake.

At least the first two decades of our lives are dedicated to learning. Then we're propelled into the "working world" where these opportunities diminish. Sure, we learn on the job, but why stop the formal education process? The big yellow school bus pulls up to our house and takes us to learn for years, and then one day it just stops. Companies need to assume that role.

Training is as necessary as a road map in an unfamiliar place. Why let your people take a wrong turn, when providing them with information will lead them where they need to go? Providing them with the *best possible* information will get them where they need to be quickly, accurately, and with pride.

In any industry or any company training is essential, but when you're providing service, it's everything because you only get one chance. The people providing it can't just go that "extra mile." They need to know which is the best direction.

The programs we've found successful can easily be adapted to fit your company's environment, needs, and goals. Hopefully, these concepts will spark some fresh ideas.

Plato Would Be Proud
Philosophical Training Programs

When we first established our training organization, we recognized the ongoing need only for technical training. It wasn't until after we had developed our technical programs that we realized there was a need for training beyond the technical.

We saw an interesting phenomenon unfold. We found we were spending a great deal of time on the intangibles of service. Most of our people's questions were hypothetical, situational, and philosophical. Those questions flagged a need, and we began to add philosophical training.

People wanted to learn the philosophy behind service as much as the mechanics. When you think about it, culture and attitude have as much effect on service as skill. Training really has to begin with philosophy.

From Parsley to Relaxation Exercises
A Seminar Program for the Whole Individual

We're not running a spa at Rosenbluth, although you might think we were if you walked into some of our seminars. A recent program we conducted on stress management found associates across the country sitting in silence, breathing deeply, thinking about the most pleasant experience of their lives or the most peaceful setting they could imagine.

The room was silent. As I closed my eyes I could feel the tension of the day slipping into the past. I envisioned clear pools of cool water filled with resting lily pads, under a clear sky. I imagined the smell of freshly cut grass and spring flowers.

I was on an island with nothing around but gentle waves lapping up on powder-white sand. I felt everything in slow motion and nothing mattered, nothing waited, only the future stretching before me.

Then the unspeakable happened. I heard a voice on my island—it was the seminar instructor. Even though he was talking about relaxation, he was bringing me back to reality and that was a cruel awakening. You could see that everyone felt the same way. But we knew we had each learned the way to our own special hideaway where we can wrap ourselves in relaxation.

Do we really do this type of thing in the middle of the workday? Yes. We were learning exercises that can lower heart rates, reduce stress, and improve health. This session is part of our monthly "Live the Spirit" seminar program.

The idea is to offer material that benefits our people's personal as well as professional lives: topics like handling difficult situations, effective speech and lasting impressions, facing change, goal setting, food and fitness, and recycling.

The Live the Spirit seminars are for all associates. A new topic is presented each month in all offices, nationwide. So we're all learning the same things together, though we're spread out over four hundred offices.

These sessions are led by Rosenbluth "service leaders," who are selected from volunteers to conduct these programs for their offices. Service leaders come from all parts of our company, regardless of position, geographical location, or line of business.

Our training department provides them with instructions in educational techniques and small group facilitation. They are then trained each month on the specific topic to be presented. Each seminar is prepared for them by our training department, but our service leaders are encouraged to add their own personalities, stories from their own offices, and other special touches that make the seminar more personal.

One of our most popular sessions is "Perception vs. Reality." Participants discuss the importance of perception and of recognizing that other people's perceptions will differ from their own. We illustrate this through the following exercise.

The class divides into pairs and one part is blindfolded; the other is not. Containers of substances are placed before them. The blindfolded people can only touch the substance. Their partners can only look at it. Each person takes a guess as to what the substance is, and rarely are they in agreement. We use substances that could easily be mistaken. For instance, flour looks and feels like talcum powder; salt looks and feels like sugar. Some are easier to tell by touch and others by sight.

It's a tangible way to illustrate that others may see us, or something we do or say, from a completely different perspective. We emphasize that the viewpoints of others must be considered valuable, especially those of our clients, associates, and loved ones.

The Live the Spirit seminar program has proven to be very effective for us. First, *everyone* participates *every* month, so in addition to reaching everyone it also brings together people who may not normally have the opportunity to work together. The vice president of technology might be paired with someone in human resoures; someone in maintenance might sit next to someone in accounting; or someone in our ticket delivery department might role-play with one of our meeting planners.

Second, everyone across the country learns about the same subject at the same time. So the program initiates talk among our people, which extends the learning process beyond the seminar itself.

Third, the program gives the fifty volunteer service leaders an opportunity to express themselves in a way they might not normally do in their day-to-day work. This grooms future leaders.

Most important, the seminar topics are submitted by our associates. It's a great way for them to express their developmental needs, their concerns, and their interests and to see the company helping to meet those needs.

Time is the only resource of significance required for such a program, but the commitment is sizable. Our fifty volunteer "Live the Spirit" trainers each commit four weeks per year (one each quarter) to learning and customizing the material, preparing and arranging for the seminars, conducting them, and soliciting feedback from those who attended. That equates to 7,500 person-hours per year, just for the instructors.

Attendance at the seminars is considered mandatory but it's not enforced, nor does it need to be. People like attending. The programs stand on their own merit and attendance is extremely high.

To make the math a little easier, let's use an attendance rate of 100 percent. The programs are held each month and each seminar lasts about an hour. So if all 2,600 people attend, that comes to 31,200 hours per year spent attending "Live the Spirit" seminars. But we've found those to be hours well spent, and we're convinced the program is worth our investment.

Other Starters in the All-Star Lineup
A Sampling of Programs

We have a number of philosophical training programs and I won't cover them all, but I'll outline a few and explain their objectives. These sessions are optional and available to everyone, though some are geared toward somewhat specific audiences. The only requirement for attendance is that each person can work them into her schedule while not negatively impacting service to our clients or placing an unreasonable burden on fellow associates.

These programs are in demand. People really look forward to attending them, and in many cases there is a waiting list for the sessions. If you stand back and look at what we're doing, I'm sure you'll see ways in which these programs could be applied in any business today.

Professional Development Seminars are offered to all associates on a periodic basis. They are taught by associates throughout the company who have expertise in a particular area such as public speaking, business writing, time management, innovation, and other general business skills.

The programs are participatory—the attendees have to give a speech to the group in public speaking and draft business letters in the writing course. I'll walk you through one—our Professional Development Seminar on innovation. This program was created by my brother, Lee, our chief operating officer, along with our director of training.

Ready to get a jolt of creativity, the participants are met with a pop quiz with questions like "What's the name of the conference room we're in?" (These sessions are usually held in a hotel meeting space.) Or, "Can you describe what the facilitator is wearing without looking?" Or it might ask, "Who's the editor in chief of your hometown paper?"

The questions are designed to make people realize that there's a lot of information all around them—the same information that surrounds us all. But the difference is that some people let it come through their brain's "filter," where they can do something with it, and others don't. There's a big difference between seeing things and going about our business and really observing things and acting upon what we have learned.

Next is a problem-solving exercise in which each person is given a Rubik's Cube. Two of the cubes are just two turns away from being solved, and it's especially interesting to watch the people with those cubes. One out of two usually makes a disaster of his cube and the other solves it right away. The message is that so often we are close to a solution, but we forge ahead without stopping for a moment to assess where we are and where we want to be.

It's also interesting to watch people's reactions to their neighbor arriving at the solution. People very seldom will ask the person who succeeded for help—another common mistake in business and life.

The facilitator usually stands in front of the group, noticeably peeling the colored stickers off the cube and placing them where he wants them to be. Some people never look up or notice. Others claim, "You aren't supposed to do that." At the end, the instructor asks, "Why not use an unconventional method to solve the problem? No one said my solution was against the rules. My instructions were merely to solve the puzzle so that the colors were grouped together." Sometimes there's a viable shortcut to solving a problem.

A presentation on heroes of innovation proves that even the great ones guess wrong. Around here, everyone's favorite example is the story of a meeting between my grandfather, Joseph Rosenbluth, and an airline sales rep in the 1930s. At the end of the meeting, Joseph said to him, "Son, get into another line of work. The commercial airline business will never amount to anything."

The facilitator holds up products, one by one, and asks the participants what happened to each of them. There are usually a lot of nostalgic faces in the crowd when they see things like a record album (since replaced by 8-tracks, cassettes, and compact disks) and a wooden tennis racquet (displaced by aluminum, graphite, and now, the oversized version). The point is that no company can coast on just one key product. They must keep reinventing themselves or someone else will invent them right out of existence.

In an exercise to get the creative juices flowing, small groups convene and try to come up with as many alternative uses as they can for a particular household product, usually something like a tea bag. Lipton would never have imagined their product could be used to do everything from being worn as an earring to saving the world.

After the groups share their ideas, the program concludes with a serious discussion about specific ideas each person feels can increase the level of innovation and creativity in their department or office. And as follow-up, each participant receives a list of the ideas contributed by all who have attended in the past.

Our *Leadership Skills* training program is designed for associates who are in, or are about to enter, leadership positions within the company. It addresses the specific skills needed for leadership, such as problem-solving, the allocation of resources, the development of people, the art of motivating, and other skills that don't always feel comfortable at first.

The program centers around active learning and includes homework, self-assessment, individual projects, and group problem-solving. Each person develops a specific action plan for his or her own further leadership development.

Everyone who enters the program attends an intial session on what leadership means in our company. Then the seventy-hour program is broken into modules so people can attend those sessions that cover areas in which they need development.

Another program, *Leadership Development,* is a sort of apprenticeship designed to groom well-rounded leaders for the future. A handful of people are selected each year, either from outside the company or within, and are placed in key departments throughout the organization for a few months at a time over an eighteen-month period. It's similar to the rotation concept in medical residency programs.

The program helps us to deepen our bench of leaders, which is invaluable in a dynamic environment, particularly in times of rapid growth. We have to be able to get programs and services off the ground quickly. With leaders in the wings we can do it.

While our management trainees contribute to each department, they're learning a great deal about the company from a variety of perspectives. Upon completion of their eighteen-month commitment to the program they can usually write their own ticket.

Where are they now? The people who have gone through the program are in leadership positions throughout the company. One was selected to open our Pacific Rim headquarters in Singapore and is living there now. Another orchestrates the implementation of new accounts across the country.

Others still are completing their "rotations," preparing us for the future.

From Novice to Pro
Comprehensive Technical Training

Most companies have technical training, so I've focused on the philosophical aspects of our training. But there are facets of our technical training that can also have broad applications to businesses outside our industry.

I'll use our training programs for reservationists for illustration, because they make up most of our company. Every industry has its own parallel position—frontline people who work with clients on a day-to-day basis. We require all reservationists, no matter their level of expertise, to participate in our technical training program. Depending upon their level of experience, that ranges from 48 to 320 hours of instruction.

When people start at square one they move from our New Associate Orientation straight into our eight-week training program to teach them the process from scratch. They don't show up at their workplace until they have successfully completed the course.

This program enables us to lessen our dependence upon our industry to provide a labor source. We try to hire as many people as we can locally, to become part of the communities in which our clients are based. Our training gives us a competitive advantage because we can do that without worrying about finding people with prior travel experience.

We are able to hire the type of person who will excel in our culture and provide our clients with the service to which they have become accustomed. The technical can be learned. Our training program ensures that we will always have qualified reservationists.

We do hire a number of people with experience as well, but they too must complete technical training. Even those with extensive experience in corporate reservations still are not ready to serve our clients. We have our way of doing things, our own style of service which includes elegant language, the use of our proprietary technology, and knowledge of our clients' corporate travel policies. We teach these and other aspects of our service in our "conversion" class.

All reservationists participate in recurrent training to keep up with technological enhancements, industry trends, and client needs. No industry or company is exempt from the need to provide ongoing training to keep people current.

TLC
The Role of Leader as Coach

It's imperative that on-the-job training occur daily. We refer to it as "coaching" because that's the relationship we seek to emulate in our training. On an athletic team, the players possess raw talent. The coach's job is to refine that talent, bring it to its fullest potential, and coordinate the talents of all of the members so that the individual contributions complement each other for the success of the entire team.

Coaching in the workplace is the exact same concept. The workplace is the playing field, the coaches are your leaders, and the team members are your people.

Coaching is important for every person, every day, but nowhere is it more vital than for new people. They can't be thrown from the training room to their workstation to fend for themselves. They should be coached by experienced people, to encourage them and guide them through situations that weren't presented in training.

They say true life is stranger than fiction. There will

always be a need or idiosyncrasy you couldn't anticipate in preparing your people to serve your clients. There's no end to the variety in people's needs, wants, and tastes. Experienced people need to be accessible to share their knowledge with those less experienced.

The philosophical and technical training of these new associates is followed by two months of on-the-job instruction provided by experienced coaches. We call this our Transitional Learning Center (TLC). Though this is part of our training for new reservationists, the concept of a transitional learning program could be utilized in any department of any organization to ease new hires into the mainstream.

2,200 Computers Later
Training by Challenge

Not all training programs are formalized. People learn by example and through experience, so you need to ensure that those examples and experiences are the ones you want to reinforce. If you continually provide a variety of projects, people will rise to the occasion and develop new talents. In fact, without being challenged, people may never discover a talent they possess—and that's a crime.

Change is a great motivator to learn new things. But it's vital to provide security so people won't fear change. New products and new ways of doing things don't replace people. Lack of training in these new things does. As leaders, it's our responsibility to provide that training.

Today, technology is a part of our everyday lives. We do most of our banking through ATMs, but a decade ago, people didn't trust computers on the street to manage their financial transactions. We conduct a large portion of our business via fax, voice mail, and electronic mail. Annoyingly enough, computers even call us on the phone during dinner trying to sell us something.

I remember when technology invaded our workplace and everyone was afraid that somehow computers would replace them. They resisted using them, but at the same time, saw their inevitability. We broke down fear by assuring our people that whatever our company did and however we did it, they would play an important part. But in order to do so they had to embrace change. To help them do that, we provided thorough training on our new computer systems. And today, four mainframes and 2,200 personal computers later, we're fully automated and a better company for it.

Our distribution methods may change, but our people will always come first. Loyalty to our company is high—in part because our people know that rather than hiring new people to use the new products, we train our own associates to use our new products. That's not only job security; it's an endless opportunity to learn new things.

Connoisseur Clients
Educating Your Clients About Your Business

For companies that provide excellent products and services, the most educated client is the best client. The reason is simple: The more your clients know about your industry, the more they will be able to appreciate the service you provide. To the less discerning, all products and services may look alike, and the full value of what you provide can be missed.

For that reason, we offer training for our clients as well, some formal, some informal. Topics might range from how to create the best travel and entertainment policy to international travel safety to hands-on applications of our technology products. Some of the topics are requested by our clients and others are offered because we see a trend developing in our industry.

Aside from these seminars, we offer informal training via communication vehicles, such as newsletters and client briefings. We invite educated comparisons to our competitors because we want our clients to understand the true value of our service.

From Travel Agent to Teacher
A Learning Organization Calls for Original People

To be able to teach the wide variety of programs we envisioned, we knew we needed a department dedicated specifically to training. We chose the team carefully, knowing it would have the same effect on people's lives that teachers do.

There are certain backgrounds that lend themselves to training. Teaching experience and training within another company are ideal credentials, but we don't limit ourselves there. We've also found that a theater background can prepare someone beautifully for a corporate training role.

We've discovered some strong trainers by promoting from within. We rely more upon personality traits than specific backgrounds when selecting people for training positions. The best traits are poise, polish, outstanding communication skills, a sense of humor, and enthusiasm. It's also essential that each and every trainer be a role model.

Today, we have a full-time training staff of twenty-seven, and twelve centers around the country dedicated to learning. In addition to creating and presenting a wide variety of programs, our training department serves as a resource for the company. Our trainers facilitate meetings and create customized learning tools whenever the need arises.

It's important to look at training as a long-term investment. Companies that look for immediate returns on the time and money spent on training will be disappointed. The investment in training should be viewed no differently from any capital project. Its success should be gauged by the benefits over the entire life of the project, not just by looking at years one and two. Similarly, trainers shouldn't have to waste time trying to justify the investment. Their time should be spent developing and conducting learning programs. And time and resources must be committed toward *their* continual development as educators.

Learning Frontiers
A Way to Share What We Have Learned

We attribute much of our success to our training philosophy and programs. We believe that our approach to learning magnifies the contributions of our people, makes our business more profitable, and helps us achieve our goals.

Some years ago clients began asking if they could sit in on our training programs. They began to ask how we developed them. It was companies with excellent training initiatives themselves that were asking. We were honored, but we were also surprised.

Eventually, our training team was spending so much of

their time explaining our programs that they had little time to develop and teach new ones. We became concerned. We put our heads together and decided that if there was that much interest, perhaps we should make our training available to outside companies. So we began a new line of business we call "Learning Frontiers."

All of our philosophical training programs are offered through Learning Frontiers—the ones explained earlier and many more. The programs most frequently requested seem to be those involving the building of our culture, our people-first focus, and service. We call them "The Creation, Care and Feeding of Corporate Values" and "Today's Orientation."

We didn't create seminars for sale. We've been successfully applying them internally for years. They've been tested and refined. We don't just refine them because we are marketing them to outside companies, we do it so they will be effective for internal use as much as external application.

The people who create and facilitate these programs continually research their topics and keep current with reading materials on the subject. They attend outside seminars and remain on top of general business issues to make sure our programs address what's important to people and companies.

It's important to the people presenting the seminars for the material to be fresh and challenging. In order to ensure that, they have to change it frequently. The facilitators constantly try new activities and add new material to their programs. And, quite simply, they keep what works and replace parts that seem "tired" with something new and original. Best of all, the programs are part of a real business and so are the trainers. They're not removed from the day-to-day challenges we all face.

The style of teaching is just as important as the content. When you break it down, you find that adults enjoy learning the way kids do, and they learn better that way. Our Learning Frontiers team emphasizes interaction, creativity, and variety in their presentation style. But there's plenty of muscle to the programs.

A key part of every seminar is the specific work plan each person completes to put to work what he or she has just learned. In fact, we suggest to participants that they not return to their offices until they've met with their people to discuss the implementation of that plan. Too many times we go away and learn great things, but when we return to the workplace we get too busy to ever use them.

The point of explaining Learning Frontiers is that if your company does something that your clients, suppliers, or colleagues are interested in, then I suggest you share it— as a new line of business.

Well Worth the Investment
A Look at Training's Bottom Line

Training isn't free, in any sense of the word. Quality training doesn't have to be exorbitant, but it takes commitment of time and money. And time *is* money when you're taking people away from their work for training.

But there is a payoff. Training benefits both the front and bottom lines. How else can you bring out the talents in your people and prepare them and your company for tomorrow and years to come? Training provides a more proficient work force, improves quality, and cements loyalty.

Training Tips to Consider
A *Summary*

- Consider training an essential part of your company. It means the difference between success and failure in the service industry, and more and more manufacturing companies are finding the competitive battleground is becoming one of service.
- Remember the kindergarten principle: *Make learning fun.* People retain more when information is presented in a creative, interactive, and interesting manner.
- Training must be attitudinal as well as technical, and it must be perpetual. Culture and attitude are as important to service as skill is.
- Try offering training programs on general subjects, to all of your people, on a regular basis. It creates cohesiveness and consistency and fosters teamwork. Offer material that benefits the personal and professional lives of your people. You'll be pleased with the results.
- A program to teach leadership *skills* (such as mastery of performance reviews, problem solving, etc.) can be extremely valuable in preparing people who have been newly promoted or those who join your company in a leadership position.
- A leadership development program can be an excellent way to groom future leaders. It's similar to a medical residency program, in which each person spends a couple of months at a time in each department. The in-

dividuals, the departments, and the company all benefit.

- Continually sharpen your technical training and be sure it's comprehensive enough to enable you to hire people with no experience in your particular field. This will broaden the scope of people from which you hire—a distinct human resource advantage.

- Offer a "conversion" training class to even the most experienced new hires to confirm their level of expertise. It ensures that they'll do business the way *your company* does, not the way their previous employers did business.

- Always provide training for your people for new products or methods you plan to employ in your company. This will eliminate the need to find new people to use these products and will go a long way to ensure that your people won't resist change as a result of fear.

- Try training by challenge. Your people will surprise themselves and you with what they are capable of doing when challenged. Provide a variety of new projects and employ new tools. People will develop new skills to rise to the challenges.

- Daily coaching of your people by their leaders will strengthen the skills of both. It's particularly important for those new on the job. You may want to consider creating a Transitional Learning Center to ease new hires into the mainstream. Take a tip from the player-coach relationship in sports. The coach orchestrates the play of the game to bring out the talents of each individual for the success of the team as a whole. That's leadership.

- In selecting your training staff, consider people with theater backgrounds as well as those with experience in teaching and corporate training. Grooming your own trainers by promoting from within can also be very effective. Be sure to offer ongoing training to your trainers, too.

- In addition to training specialists, involve people throughout your organization in training—it allows them to use talents not often exercised. It's also a great way to spot potential leaders.

- Training your clients will help them to see the true value of your products and services in the context of the marketplace. The more they know about your industry the easier it will be for them to differentiate you from your competitors. They become connoisseurs of your service.

- Commit the training resources necessary for your company—both financial and in terms of time. It's a long-term investment that you'll never regret.

CHAPTER 7

TECHNOLOGY AS A TOOL

You can't just give a carpenter a hammer and ask him to build a house. A doctor can't provide treatment to patients with only a stethoscope. Every artisan must have all the right tools at her disposal in order to do her very best.

Technology is an essential tool in virtually every business today. There probably isn't anything a computer can do that a person can't. It's people who give computers their intelligence anyway. But the secret is time.

Calculations can be generated, geometric designs drawn, and documents produced, but without computers, what we accomplish today would take an impossible amount of person-hours—resources we can't afford to waste.

Technology allows us to accomplish more in the time we are given, and makes otherwise tedious work automatic, thereby freeing our time to create. It's a tremendous tool. But for many, technology is intimidating, cause for insecurity, perhaps seen as a potential replacement for people. Technology should be used to empower our people and our clients.

In his newsletter, *On Achieving Excellence,* Tom Peters said, "Rosenbluth Travel has redefined a mundane business through an astonishing array of proprietary software that helps corporate clients track and manage their costs." In the same article he also writes, "The 'elegant service' is as significant as the software. While beating the Joneses on information technology is essential, failing to implement through people would be a disaster."

Reaching Out and Not Touching Anyone
Learning from a Failed Product

Not all technology products will make the hall of fame. In 1983, we created one we called "REACHOUT®" and it fizzled. It transmitted air schedules and hotel and car information to clients' desktop computers. We made significant investments to build the system and we never got a return on our investment.

The problem was that we didn't understand the difficulty our clients had in using the product. The people who developed and tested it were accustomed to using it, but they weren't the ones we developed it for. We blindly supported the product because we believed the marketplace needed it. We learned our lesson, and we put a lot more listening behind the development of products today.

There was a silver lining to that dark cloud. REACH-OUT served as a platform for the development of a very powerful product, "E-Res™." It allows our clients to send us travel requests through their electronic mail systems, and there is a significant demand for this product.

To develop the right products, we have to keep an ear to the ground to know what's coming, and we have to listen to both our clients and our people. We don't necessarily have to get to the marketplace first with our products. We just have to be the best.

To provide a map of our information systems landscape, I'll divide it into three primary areas: the front room, middle room, and back room. I'll discuss selected products of each. While in our case they pertain to travel, what they offer has application to virtually any industry.

THE FRONT ROOM

There are many differences between our technology and that of our competitors, and this becomes clear when we are bidding for an account. We put much of our emphasis on our front-room investments and capabilities, while our competitors seem to hype back-end quality control. It stems from our philosophy that getting things right the first time is more efficient, less expensive, and above all, more convenient for our clients. We want our customers to be able to make one call and then forget about their travel plans.

We designed our system to build in customization and quality checks up front, where the reservations are made. We don't want to have to keep calling clients back to ask for information or correct an error found in a final quality check. On occasion we still have to, but the emphasis we have placed on, and the investments we have put into, our front-room system make it a rare occurrence. Let's take a look at two key front-room products that give us the power to serve our clients the way we want to. They're READOUT and PRECISION℠.

Solving a Communication Lag
A Product to Get the Lowest Fare

In 1983, we created a product called READOUT. I mentioned it earlier, in Chapter 4, but I didn't tell you much about it.

After airline deregulation we were seeing sometimes hundreds of thousands of airfare changes a day. Each airline had its own reservations system, and while the systems included the flights of every airline, there was lag time in updating information between the systems. If an airline changed its fares it would update its own system first, and within twenty-four to forty-eight hours those rates would register in the other systems.

We saw that our clients could miss out on the lowest fares because of that delay. So we leased every available system, put them side by side, and compared the rates. From that manual process, we created our own private system.

It meshes the information from all of the systems and lists the airfares in ascending order according to price. Our reservationists never have to search for the lowest fare; READOUT lists it first. For nearly a decade now, READ-OUT has enabled our clients to use airfare changes to their advantage.

For years, a team of associates came to work at 5:00 A.M. each day to check the airfare changes and load them into the system. Recently that process was automated, so now those associates can sleep a little later. Their role has shifted to providing support with complex faring issues. Automating READOUT not only removed the chance for human error, it freed some creative associates from tedious work so their time can be spent helping our people and our clients in a more hi-touch way.

Stress Buster/Service Enhancer
A Product Based upon Conditional Logic

The reservations process is the foundation of our service. It directly impacts the highest number of people in our clients' organizations. It takes place twenty-four hours a day, three hundred sixty-five days a year. This process has become increasingly complicated since deregulation of the airlines in the 1970s. Prederegulation reservations had a handful of components: typically the name of the caller, name of the traveler, address, phone number, and flight plans.

Today, a single reservation has up to one hundred components, including everything from the basics to frequent flyer numbers, special meal requirements, and sort codes for all types of travel management reports. This complexity makes a higher level of service possible. But it also presents additional opportunities for error. Since our company issues about three million tickets a year, we're always looking for ways to ensure that these possibilities for error don't materialize.

But stress is just as formidable an enemy as error. Most trips require multiple reservations before the traveler's final plans are really final. That factor, added to the volume and complexity, places tremendous pressure on our people.

A few years ago, a pair of associates—one from operations and one from technology—were discussing the reservations process and asking themselves, "How can we do this better?" The result was a product we named PRECI-SION.

Our PRECISION product automates a majority of the reservations process through the use of conditional logic. This virtually eliminates opportunity for error and gives the reservationist time to offer personalized service.

There are three key areas to satisfy in any reservation: (1) adhering to the client's company travel policy; (2) honoring the personal travel preferences of the individual traveler; and (3) capturing information for client reports. PRECISION uses "if/then" steps to guide the reservation process, automatically accomplishing the three goals. Since our client's travel policy is programmed into PRECISION, the reservationist knows the client's company will allow her to fly business class to London.

Her seats can be assigned in the aisle seat she wants, her frequent flyer numbers are automatically entered, and she will receive the vegetarian meal she prefers. And meanwhile, all pertinent information is being captured and stored in our system for our client's travel management reports.

In addition to automating information, the conditional logic prompts the reservationist to the next step. For example, if a person books outgoing and returning flights for different dates, PRECISION automatically shows hotel and rental car choices for that city that meet the client company's policy requirements.

This product has saved our clients and our company a significant amount of time. The reservations process is faster and more accurate. The quality is enhanced. PRECISION has increased productivity, driven down costs, and created demand for our service.

The benefits of a conditional logic tool speak for themselves. Each company has its own processes that cry out to be automated. The company benefits from the productivity gains, but the client is the real winner. Detailed customer profiles can be entered into systems to help a company personalize its service. And its people are elevated from the tedious to the nurturing aspects of service.

A Two-Way Street
Good Products Aren't Created in a Vacuum

Our technology wizards don't create their products in a vacuum. They are constantly in touch with our clients and associates, seeking input on what they need. For example, when PRECISION was developed, focus groups of future users designed what they wanted it to do.

But the input didn't stop there. An evaluation mechanism was entered into PRECISION that allows our reservationists to comment to its creators as they use the program, while the suggestions are fresh in their minds. These evaluations lead to continual enhancements of the product.

THE MIDDLE ROOM

The middle room serves as a filter process, where we make sure that our clients' needs and requests are fulfilled. Even though our front-room systems ensure accuracy up front, not all client preferences are available at the time of booking, and we can't stop there. We need a system that keeps trying. That's our middle room. We call our key middle-room product ULTRAVISION, and it performs a variety of functions.

Ultravision

An Automated Quality Assurance Program

The primary feature of ULTRAVISION is automated quality assurance. In addition to double-checking that all the basics of a reservation are correct, it also makes sure that no schedule changes have occurred, and if they have, the system sends a message to the reservationist, who then calls the client with the information.

Another key function of ULTRAVISION is to ensure that the lowest airfare was obtained. If for any reason it was not (such as if the fare was sold out at the time the reservation was made), the reservation is automatically wait-listed until that fare becomes available. When the fare opens up, a message containing the new information is cued to the reservationist. If no lower fare is found or a lower fare doesn't become available, a message indicating this is added to the record.

ULTRAVISION does the same with seats. Everyone has that favorite seat—bulkhead or near an exit, window or aisle. And nobody wants a middle seat. This can be a big frustration for travelers. The system automatically checks to verify that each client's preferred seat is obtained, and if it's not or if no seats are booked, an error message is sent to the reservationist. If the preferred seats are available they are automatically booked and the change is cued. If they are not, the client is wait-listed for her special seat until the flight departs.

Our middle room also makes pretrip travel management information available to clients by extracting it from our database of future itineraries. Our clients use this information for three purposes.

The first is risk management. For instance, companies

can pull the records of those planning travel to international destinations that have been placed on security alert by the State Department, so they can make alternative plans.

The second is adherence to company travel policy. Information on any arrangements made outside of the client's guidelines can be reviewed by the company's travel administrator and acted upon before the travel takes place.

The third purpose to pull pretravel information is for negotiations with suppliers for group travel rates. Whenever ten or more passengers from the same company travel on the same carrier to the same destination, they are usually entitled to group rates. But they can only take advantage of it if they know they've reached the required numbers.

I've told you about the various functions this product performs, but I haven't quantified what it does. ULTRA-VISION checks every component in up to two thousand reservations per hour. That's a lot of work that, in the past, took a lot of people a great deal of time to do.

Automating the quality assurance process can heighten quality, customize service, increase productivity, and strengthen client confidence for any company. It's another tool to hand off stress to a machine so people are free to do what machines can't.

THE BACK ROOM

I mentioned our independence in the back room in Chapter 4, but just to refresh your memory, we made a decision about a decade ago to take a strategic leap in the area of information management. Instead of subscribing to an airline's back-room system, as most agencies do, we decided to invest in our own system and programmers. This gave us freedom to use information in ways it had never been used before in our industry—ways that brought enormous benefit to our clients.

We were limited with the airline system. There were clear-cut boundaries on what we could and couldn't do with a system and programming staff that weren't our own. When a client asked us to do something unique, we often had to say "no," and that got under our skin. Now we can always at least say "maybe," and usually "yes."

Our people are always eager and proud to tell me about meetings with clients where multiple agencies are represented. Because when the topic gets to technology and the client asks around the room which agency can achieve a certain technological goal the client has set, usually our people are the only ones in the room who unequivocally say "yes." They like that and so do the clients.

Vision
The Nuts and Bolts

We call our back-room system VISION®, and it houses a database of information collected from all of our locations worldwide. The system holds information on all travel activity for more than a year at a time. This data is vital in negotiating with suppliers on behalf of our clients.

Using this information, we can also help our clients direct travel to the most cost-effective alternatives for their company, in terms of carriers, hotels, car rental companies, times of day, and days of week to travel. The system is supported by a twenty-four-hour-a-day, seven-day-a-week operations and engineering staff. And it has backup upon backup, daily off-site storage of information, and a multi-tiered password system for security.

What Does It Do?
Benefits of a Privately Owned Back-Room System

One of the most popular features of our VISION data center is "data download," which allows our clients to extract their company's data from our system, on a monthly basis, and store it in their own computers. There, they can accumulate it each month and keep year-to-date figures at their fingertips.

There is no charge for data downloads, and along with them we provide a one-day training class for our clients, a comprehensive training manual, and a toll-free hotline to answer any data-related questions. If clients prefer, they can access our system on-line and pull their company's data into their personal computers for immediate access to nationally consolidated information, current up to the previous day's ticketing.

Corporate Marriage at Its Best
Integrating Information Systems with Clients

The concept of "corporate marriage" is discussed in Chapter 13, "Open Partnerships." The term applies to a union between a company's people and those of its clients, on a multilevel basis. The same union can take place in technology. Two instances in which we mesh our system with those of our clients are payroll updates and credit card reconciliation.

We had a meeting with a very large account in which thirty-four divisions of the company were represented. Each had a totally different structure, set of travel guidelines and reporting requirements, and they wanted us to be familiar with them all and to serve each traveler in each division accordingly. It was a logistical nightmare.

After five hours, we came up with a solution that has made life a lot easier and service a lot better. We developed a program with that client to interface with their human resources database, which includes the most current information in all of the areas needed.

Now, in order to access the travel policy, reporting requirements, department number, and a host of other information needed for each traveler, all our reservationist needs is the caller's social security number. This lessens the amount of time needed for both the reservationist and the client at the point of sale, and ensures that we are working with up-to-the-minute information. Since that time, we have instituted this program with at least twenty additional clients.

Along the same lines, we have begun interfacing with our clients' accounting systems to perform corporate credit card reconciliations for their travel expenditures. This saves our clients tremendous amounts of time because it eliminates the need for their people to manually reconcile their statements each month.

We produce reports that indicate charges that matched, credit card charges for which we have no travel record, and travel records for which no charge has been posted to their credit card. The reports serve as accountant and auditor for our clients so their companies don't have to.

SURROUNDVISION
The Story of a "Make or Break" Product

We have a client in California who has awarded 60 percent of its business to our company and has a contract with a local agency for the remaining 40 percent. Our client has very sophisticated technology needs, which the smaller agency is unable to meet. So we came up with a solution that is being scrutinized by our industry.

We offered to consolidate the smaller agency's travel information with our own, to provide our client comprehensive data on their entire travel account. This is no easy task. First, it's risky to become the gatekeeper for another agency's information—travel arrangements we didn't make. Second, it's vital that this data not fall into our own general ledger activity.

This has never been done before. Our technology associates have written a program to provide the interface, while keeping the accounting information separate. They call their new program SURROUNDVISION, because we are pulling information from outside our company into our own database.

If we succeed, we will make history in our industry and open up a world of opportunity in serving clients who choose to contract their business to multiple agencies— and there are many. And by charging a transaction fee to the agencies whose data we are handling, we will be able to recoup our investment over time.

The Information Broker
Recognizing the Power of Information

Information is power, and we're all information brokers. We just need to recognize it. We need to know which information to capture and how to analyze it. We have to find ways to turn that information into understanding, and ultimately, into benefits for our clients.

Our VISION system is all about providing information to our clients. The reports it generates show savings realized, but more important, they show opportunities for savings that are being missed. This enables us to work with each company to provide a plan of action to take advantage of those opportunities.

There are countless ways companies can use technology to positively impact the lives of their people and clients. The key is to get close enough to their customers to find out how to best support them. The most sophisticated hardware or software won't help a client if it doesn't address his or her particular needs.

The Fabulous Four
Technology Specialists Who Speak English

We have a department of four people dedicated to matching the specific technology needs of our clients with our technological capabilities. They explain our products to our clients in layman's terms and support them in their use.

One of these four associates, named Beth, used to receive copies of all reports before they went to our clients. She would review and correct them and send them back to be run again. Eventually, a programmer approached her and asked what it was she looked for when reviewing the reports.

He suspected the process was wasting computer time, and if he knew what she looked for, he could write a program to make those corrections before the reports were printed. He did, and the reports now come to her error-free. Since he wrote the program just for her, he began calling it the "Beth Edit," and the name stuck.

When we explain this program to our clients we call it by a much more formal name, but sometimes our technology associates slip and refer to it by their name for it. It's funny, but once clients hear it, they seem to like calling it the Beth Edit too. They all know Beth and they like the human touch the name brings to technology.

This crew does such a tremendous job of explaining our technology products that recently, when a prospective client came to our headquarters for a technology demonstration, the client conducted the demonstration herself. The company's travel manager had been learning about our information systems in order to evaluate them against our competitors', and when she brought the selection team in for a final analysis, she jumped up and said she knew our products so well she'd like to demonstrate them to her colleagues. We were awarded the account, and she's a great ambassador for our company.

Every Great Inventor Needs a Lab
Resources for Research and Development

Since our industry doesn't have its own version of an underwriters' lab, years ago we developed an "Automation

Lab" where a select group of our technology associates develop and test new products. They continually refine them according to feedback from our associates and clients.

In the lab, technology products currently on the market are analyzed and evaluated side by side. The winners are enhanced to meet the unique needs of our clients. Proprietary new products are developed, tested, and refined there.

Most companies have research and development initiatives, but they don't always set aside the space, people, and capital to make them what they could be—the power to design the future. It's tempting to apply profits entirely to the bottom line but it's essential to reinvest money in projects that keep your company ahead of the competition, and technology is a frontrunner. Without that investment, companies will lag behind.

Backseat Drivers Prohibited
Giving People the Freedom to Create

The freedom to create innovative technology products and services starts at the top and permeates a company. If you put people in a room with a low ceiling and tell them to jump as high as they can, they'll jump to the ceiling, never knowing if they could have jumped higher.

Raise that ceiling far beyond their reach and they have room to strive. Provide them with a trampoline and they will soar higher than humanly possible. Give them a pole to vault with and they'll go even higher.

This is our view of technology. We try to create an environment in which our people can realize their full potential. We provide them with tools that empower them to reach for the stars. And we let them choose the tools.

Just recently they chose a new tool, IBM's brand new, top-of-the-line AS/400, Model D80. It allows for higher security through a "mirroring" feature that automatically keeps two copies of all data for backup. And it offers significant enhancements in our clients' ability to communicate and share resources between their networks and ours.

This is just one example of ways in which we give our team the resources to make things happen quickly. They're not held back by restrictions. They're not enslaved by bureaucracy. They are limited only by their own imaginations and by the capability of the world's technology. That's a lot of space in which to work, and the results have given us a sustainable edge.

For instance, recently a number of airlines have begun to charge for excessive access to their computer reservation systems. Agencies that rely upon the airline systems began to use them to conduct fare searches, which our own system does for us. The airlines are charging a fee per keystroke over a set amount, which could add up to significant amounts of money for the agencies with which we compete. Since we utilize mostly our own system, we won't be paying nearly what our competitors will. This is merely one illustration of the power of strategic technology.

To keep ahead of the game, technology experts need to be able to run their own show, but at the same time their companies need to take an interest in what they do. People should work to understand technology so they can fully appreciate it, understand the needs of technology specialists, and talk intelligently with them about their work. To keep abreast of what's happening in technology, I read as much as possible on the subject and I meet with our technology associates frequently to gain a clearer understanding of what they're up to and how they're doing it. But I do try to sit back and let them lead the way.

I was once in a crucial meeting with a prospective client, in which a demonstration of a new technology product, still under development, was being given by one of our associates. At the end of the demonstration, the prospective client asked when the product would be complete, to which our associate replied that she felt it would never be complete.

For a moment, I regretted my backseat approach. Then she proceeded to tell the client that she and her fellow technology associates believed that no matter how much a product is refined and enhanced, there will always be room for improvement. I quickly went from upset to proud, and the prospective client (now a client) went from confused to impressed.

Happiness: The Ultimate Technology Tool
Special Significance for the People-First Theory

Our credo of happiness in the workplace has a special significance with respect to technology. It is without a doubt the fastest-growing aspect of business today. It is indispensable in both manufacturing and service industries. It touches every facet of people's lives.

The field of technology is fiercely competitive, and to keep pace with its changes takes special skill that is fervently sought by companies around the world. Attracting and retaining technology associates is a challenge of its own kind, beyond our ardent search for the right associates for our company.

Turnover in any company is costly, both financially and emotionally, but perhaps more so in technology. The development of products takes time, and turnover creates delays in the introduction of those products. By the time you've searched for, hired, and trained the person to take over the development of an abandoned product, it's often too late. Someone else beats you to the marketplace. Not only do you lose that opportunity, but the initial work on the product becomes a complete waste.

Delays in technological developments can be devastating. Turnover is disruptive. The nation competes vigorously for qualified and creative technology specialists, and companies end up in costly bidding wars.

We feel we've found a solution in our people-first policy. Our technology associates are very much a part of our company, unlike so many companies in which the technology department winds up like an isolated island within an organization. We involve our technology associates in all aspects of our company and seek to have people throughout the company involved in technology. This helps them to develop the *right* products for our associates and our clients. It unites technology with the rest of our company and it goes a long way toward happiness in the workplace.

The Dream Machine
Technology as a Company Hero

Our people cheer on our technology group because they create the products that make us look good for our clients. They give us a competitive advantage. The products they design empower us to do a better job, to do things our competitors can't, and to provide our clients with services they never expected.

Our technology team earned the nickname "The Dream

Machine" because they develop tools for our people that relieve stress and enhance service. That's important in any business. The more steps of a process that can be automated, the better. We have found it critical in our business.

Travelers are demanding. They usually make their plans on short notice, yet the particulars of their trip are really important to them. Often it seems that as soon as our reservationists get everything confirmed according to the travelers' wishes, their plans change suddenly and the process begins again. It's just a fact of life. It comes with the territory, and our reservationists have to have the nerves of air traffic controllers, while at the same time looking for ways to enhance service, making it special.

A lot goes into our service, though you might not realize it when you look at a ticket. Our clients see only the end result, but our people work hard to make it happen, and they couldn't do it without the tools that turn the impossible into the possible.

Technology Tips for Your Company to Consider
A Summary

- Look for methods by which technology can save time in your company, freeing your people to create and to concentrate on the finer, more intangible aspects of service. Automating mundane processes can remove opportunities for error, reduce stress, and improve service.

- Three examples of technology products we employ that may have application to your company are: (1) the use of conditional logic to automate much of what you do;

(2) an automated quality assurance program which will heighten accuracy, lower costs, and strengthen the confidence of your clients; and (3) a comprehensive data base of customer activity for your use and theirs.

- The development of technology products—as with all products, programs, and services—must not take place in a vacuum. Build in evaluation mechanisms that encourage input on the spot, while the users' suggestions are fresh in their minds.

- Consider the creation of an automation lab in which products that apply to your industry can be developed, tested, and refined.

- Information is power. Capture it and create ways to put it to work for your company and your clients. Companies can never stand still technologically. If you do not have the resources available for your own technology department, team up with a technology supplier who will take you into the future.

- Continually reinvest in technology, both in terms of people and the tools they need to stretch their talents beyond traditional limits. By the way, let *them* choose the tools they need.

- Let the experts run their own show, but take the time and make the effort to learn about what they do and how they do it. You will understand their needs more clearly and be able to more fully appreciate what they do. It'll also provide guidance in the technology project priority-setting process.

- If you do have your own technology group, be sure to cultivate happiness in their workplace. Turnover in technology is probably more costly than turnover in other departments, because of the delays in product development that result.

- Don't let your technology department become an island within your organization—involve it in all aspects of the company. That way your technology people will be more satisfied in their work, and they will emerge with a clearer understanding of the needs their products will fill.

CHAPTER 8

SERVICE IS AN ATTITUDE, AN ART, AND A PROCESS

The 1991 movie *The Doctor* illustrated the importance of compassionate service, in a very gripping way. In the movie, a callous but mechanically highly skilled doctor becomes very ill and faces hardships others must face in the wake of his work: difficult things like pain, fear, disrespect for a person's time or feelings, and even possible death.

He is a changed man because of his experience. After struggling with himself, he realizes there's more to medicine than science. He chooses a surgeon whom he once belittled to perform his crucial operation on the basis that he is a caring person. He begins to spend time with his family and to nurture the relationships he neglected. He learns a great deal from getting a taste of his own medicine. It's an eye-opener for most of us.

We're all in the service business. Even companies in the manufacturing sector are service companies. Gone are the days when a company could merely produce and distribute products. Consumers want service surrounding those products and they'll give their business to those who provide it.

It's not easy to provide good service. There's no one way to do it. We all have to do our best to develop our own formulas for service. In this chapter, I'll share our formula with you. Then I'll break it down and analyze its components.

Attitude + Art + Process
A Formula for Service

Our formula is *Service = attitude + art + process.*

Attitude encompasses many things. Finding the right people—people who care and who want to be the best—is the core of attitude. But attitudes can be influenced by external factors. If a person who cares is placed in a noncaring environment, for example, or if her efforts to go above and beyond are foiled or discouraged, her attitude can be smothered. So good attitude is really a matter of the right person working in the right environment.

Next, *art.* Anything done with conviction, with style and flair, is art. Service is—or should be—creative. There are endless things one can do to enhance a service experience. That's one of the most exciting aspects of service. There are literally endless opportunities for improvement. There is no 100 percent, only close and closer. Service is a continuous creative pursuit—an art.

Finally, *process.* Finding the best way to do things is also perpetual, and it's incredibly important. Process makes things possible. It brings order to the components of service so that the people executing them are free to concentrate on the finer points and added touches that make service come alive. Process makes measuring progress possible, which is the key to continuous improvement. Process also facilitates consistency across a large, and particularly a growing, organization.

Service is an attitude, an art, and a process, but none of these is possible without happiness in the workplace. Service is demanding, if performed well, so it inherently breaks down if those delivering it are not happy.

ATTITUDE

Let My People Go
Giving People Room to Be Outstanding

People need to be given space to provide truly outstanding service. They must be given the freedom to create and the support and encouragement they need to do great things. We like to call this a "mental safety net."

Too many managers make the mistake of holding their people down, fearing the mistakes they might make if they are given freedom. But by doing so, they are also forgoing opportunities for potentially outstanding results. This type of manager has no place in the leadership of the coming millennium. There's no room for such a person in our organization.

We all make mistakes. Anyone willing and determined to strive for something special will probably make more mistakes than someone who provides only status quo service. But mistakes are a small price to pay for the successes that often follow failed attempts. A true test of exceptional service can be found in the actions a company or individual takes to turn mistakes into positive experiences. But when we make mistakes, even when we turn them around, we've got to feel them in our stomachs—yes, our stomachs.

I contend that providing less than stellar service should make us physically nauseated. I know that after a client tells me we've erred, I usually wind up planning our recovery strategy while drinking antacid. Some people blush uncontrollably when they're embarrassed; some people's palms sweat when they're nervous. I get sick when we mess up—I literally become physically ill.

Once I ran into a client in the airport and he shared with me his dissatisfaction over a recent trip on which it seemed everything went wrong from the start. I spent the entire flight between the air phone and the lavatory. And I'm not the only one who's affected this way. Many of my colleagues are plagued with the same consequence to one degree or another.

But as with performers or athletes who fall, the best thing they can do is pick themselves up and keep going. In providing service, we have to discipline ourselves to keep moving forward in spite of any fumbles we've made. We can only learn from them if we see them as steps to improvement.

Remaining "Busied In"
The Service Attitude at Work

The Chinese philosopher Confucius was once on a journey with his disciples through dry terrain. One of his followers discovered a hidden puddle, filled his rice bowl, and offered it to the Master. Confucius was about to raise it to his lips when he caught sight of the faces of his disciples. He emptied the bowl on the ground, saying, "It would be too much for one, too little for all of us. Let us continue our walk."

Years ago, we learned a valuable lesson about teamwork that we use as a frequent reminder of the power of group effort. It's the story of a principle we called "busied in/ busied out."

We serve our clients in teams so our people and clients can get to know one another. When a client calls to make a travel reservation, the call goes to the next available member of that company's team. Our system enables reservationists to take themselves out of the loop if they feel overloaded, and when they do it's called "busying out." When they're ready to take a call they "busy in" and return to the loop.

A couple of years ago, we started serving a new account for which the volume was greatly underestimated. Our people were swamped with calls. They felt overloaded and morale was dipping.

Our vice president of operations spent some time with the team to help ensure smooth service until we could shift additional resources to that account. While she was there she developed a theory, and asked the team to give it a try for just one week. They did, and they discovered they didn't need more people after all—and productivity and morale soared.

Here's how it worked. There were ten people dedicated to serving the account, and it seemed as though the phone never stopped ringing. Each would take several calls in rapid succession and then busy out for a breather. Let's estimate that at any one time, half of them were busied out, leaving five people to bear the burden of calls. When they busied back in they would be in a group of about five, taking calls for ten.

What was happening was that their tendency to busy out was creating an overload of work for those remaining, and when they were the ones taking calls, they were overloaded by the same burden created by their associates busying out. It was a vicious cycle.

Our vice president of operations asked the team members to stay busied in all day (with the exception of their breaks, lunch, etc.) so that the calls would be distributed among ten, as was intended, as opposed to five, which had become reality. Rather than create a cycle in which they faced an overload of work, then needed a break, *everyone* made themselves available for the right amount of work, all day.

The concept is just common sense, but when people become overwhelmed, it's easy to slip into a reactive mode rather than a proactive one. The busied-in principle instilled confidence in the team that they could manage that level of work.

The busied-in principle can take on life-and-death proportions in the military. It did for the famous *Memphis Belle*, the first B-17 bomber to finish all of its required twenty-five missions during World War II. The Eighth Air Force crew flew out of England and over Germany. Ten percent of all World War II casualties were troops who did the same.

There were ten members on the crew—the pilot, co-pilot, bombardier, navigator, engineer, radioman, tail gunner, belly gunner, and left and right waist gunners. Every position was critical. They each had a job to do and if even one person had busied out, the crew would have faced death or capture by the enemy. Every man's life rested not just on his own shoulders but on those of each fellow crew member. They all survived by staying "busied in."

While we were all glued to our sets during Operation Desert Storm, watching updates on military strategy and maneuvers, this mammoth undertaking was putting the busied-in rule to work. The supply and transportation units, medical teams, engineers, ground, air, and sea troops, and even reporters all had a job to do. Several nations, if not the world, depended on them. In these situations people simply can't let each other down.

In industry, the principle doesn't carry the same dire consequences, but it can mean the life or death of a company if people relax into letting others pull some of their weight. In the manufacturing sector, when people are busied out, it can halt production. In the airline industry, a flight is grounded until it has the proper ratio of crew to passengers. So if a flight attendant doesn't show up, the customers have to wait until a replacement arrives.

Have you ever waited in line at the supermarket or bank, and the checkout person puts up a "counter closed" sign? You know what happens next. You move to another line and wait for a very long time along with everyone else. And by the time people reach the front of the line they're steaming, and often not very pleasant to the person who *does* serve them.

There are also sports that closely parallel the service attitude we're describing. Two in particular are rowing and tug-of-war. In these two sports, everyone has to literally pull his own weight. Trust is a must. You can be rowing or pulling with all your might, but unlike other sports that more clearly demonstrate individual effort, how do you *know* each of your teammates is giving her all?

You can't know, so you have to trust, encourage each

other to be your best, and keep your goals in synch. You have to choose your teammates wisely and you have to work together to make the strengths of one offset the weaknesses of another.

The key is for us all to stay busied in, especially management. It's top leadership's role to extend the busied-in technique across departmental lines, so that companies as a whole perform like a rowing team.

ART

Frances Russell
The Story of a Service Hero

I had perhaps the best service experience of my life on a trip to San Francisco in 1989. The combination of an experience beautiful in its simplicity and completely unexpected made it what it was—and I don't think I'll ever forget it.

My wife and I stopped by a restaurant for breakfast before starting our day, expecting little except a hurried and possibly grumpy waitress, serving some pretty good eggs and very good coffee. Up walks Frances Russell, of Sears Fine Foods, the creator of an exceptional service experience. She was polite, friendly, and efficient. You could tell she took a great deal of pride in her work, and I began to see that the service would be good. But the unexpected came when she prepared to pour my coffee.

Normally, if 90 percent of your coffee in a standard restaurant lands in your cup, you're doing well. But before serving my coffee she asked if I was right-handed or left-handed. Living in a right-handed world, I was surprised to be asked, but I was even more surprised to be asked by a waitress in a restaurant. When I answered that I was left-handed, she proceeded to reposition everything on the table to be more convenient to a southpaw, including setting the coffee cup to my left and moving everything else aside.

Before that time, I was quite accustomed to moving the cup and other items myself. In fact, I was so accustomed to it that before this experience, I never even realized I was doing it! But now, Frances Russell has spoiled me for life. Every time I go into a restaurant, and my waiter or waitress assumes that I am right-handed or really doesn't care either way, I will move the items myself and think of Frances Russell.

The point is that once you have had an extraordinary service experience, nothing else will do. People shouldn't have to settle for less than outstanding service. People shouldn't *give* less than outstanding service, but the dilemma is that they most often do. That makes us appreciate it all the more when we receive truly fine service.

When you're dedicated to providing excellent service, you become jaded to the point where it begins to infringe upon your life. You become less and less tolerant of poor, even average, service. You begin to analyze the service you receive with a trained eye.

My colleagues and I may not be able to relax in a restaurant because we're too busy analyzing the service, but we think that's great. Why shouldn't we have the highest expectations of service? Why shouldn't our clients demand the best? We hope they will, and we hope we can rise to the occasion. Our goal is to spoil our clients beyond the point where anyone else's service will do.

Frances Russell is a service hero. I'm proud to say we also have a few of our own. We consistently get our clients seats on sold-out flights, rooms in sold-out hotels, and last-minute passports and visas. We try to get them complimentary upgrades to first class on flights and suites in hotels.

These perks might seem appropriate from a travel company. You may be surprised to learn that we also locate lost luggage for our clients; act as a message service, calling spouses or secretaries; greet our clients' special guests at the airport; and when our clients return from overseas, then have a coast-to-coast flight, we'll deliver their mail to them to read on the flight home. Beyond that, we often make arrangements for our clients for theater tickets, sporting events, restaurant reservations, babysitting services, golf tee times, and we even get requests for wake-up calls.

Then there are those unusual situations when we really get an opportunity to come through for our clients. In two such instances we were literally going to the dogs.

The general manager for a National Hockey League team, who is one of our clients, bought a dog as a gift for the general manager of another team. The client asked us to take care of the dog's flight arrangements. What did we do? We rented a kennel and flew the dog with a personal escort to ensure his safe arrival. Our associate delivered the dog, in person, and returned home on the next flight.

Another client had to make an emergency trip at the last minute. When he called to make his reservations, he mentioned he was worried about quickly securing someone to take care of his dogs while he was gone. Our associate spent the week dog-sitting.

A client called us at 3:00 A.M. in a panic because he was on the road and his wife was in labor. We chartered him a flight and he made it home in time for the birth of his first child.

One of our clients who suffers from severe asthma called us when an airline lost the luggage containing her medicine. Our associates were so concerned that while one traced the luggage and arranged for its immediate delivery to the hotel, another stayed on the phone with the client the entire time to make sure her breathing was stable until the medicine arrived.

Every company will have its favorite service stories. But the secret is to make this level of service the norm and not the exception. The attitude and art components of our formula are vital, but without process, it is very difficult to master service and make it routinely excellent.

PROCESS

Cook with the Best Ingredients
The Importance of Building Quality In Up Front

Just having a process won't cut it. You have to have a quality process, and it's hard work to develop one. In order for your company to operate at peak performance, there must be a quality process for everything you do.

I regret the overuse of the word *quality*, but no other word means quite the same thing. There are words that come close, but they don't accurately describe what we all strive to achieve. I guess that's why the word has been used by virtually every company to describe their products and services. I'll use it anyway because it's the best word we've got.

Quality has to be built in up front. It doesn't work to try to make up for it at the end. Quality built in, up front, to every single product, process, and service costs less, though one would think the opposite to be true. We have examples to prove it.

There's no substitute for doing it right the first time. In a company providing quality service, the need for a customer service department should be minimal if not nonexistent. We have significantly reduced ours and continue to strive to deplete the need for it, shifting those resources to more productive purposes. For quality products and services, problems and complaints are the exception, not the norm.

There's an advertising campaign that paints a clear picture of what I'm saying. You know the one: The appliance repairman bemoans his loneliness because he is never needed. The message: The company's appliances work, and if you own one you will use it for years and years without needing a repairman. Quality should be so good in America.

A person dining in a restaurant that prepares its meals with the finest ingredients will normally enjoy the meal with no additional seasoning or condiments. On the other hand, when bland or inferior ingredients are used, those dining will reach for salt and pepper and ask their waiter or waitress for mustard, catsup, horseradish, and all varieties of condiments to enhance the flavor, or lack thereof, in the food.

The same can be said for service. When quality is built in at the outset, clients have little need to ask for corrections after the fact, thus diminishing the need for a customer service department. In the end, it takes a certain number of ingredients to make up service. Why not use the right ones in the first place?

Quality Control
An Oxymoron

I think "quality control" is an oxymoron. True quality needs space to breathe. If quality is built in, then where's the need for control? Why on earth would you want to control quality? It should be allowed to run rampant.

Give your people the proper tools and freedom to use them, and in the right atmosphere, they will create and perpetuate quality.

The Right to Be Pygmalion
Tailoring a Quality Program for Your Company

In Greek mythology, Pygmalion was the king of Cyprus who carved an ivory statue of the maiden of his dreams. He fell in love with his creation and pleaded to Aphrodite, the goddess of love and beauty, to bring her to life. She granted his wish and the statue became Galatea, Pygmalion's love.

We're all Pygmalions to a certain degree. When dating, everybody's probably found themselves wishing they could take one person's personality and combine it with another person's appearance and add to that the timing of another relationship. Through this process, we'd try to create our ideal.

When selecting a home, there's that special room in one, another is in the neighborhood where we'd like to live, and then there's the question of price. We want the ideal home for the ideal price.

Of course, none of the above is possible in our world, but I have some good news. We've found that you *can* selectively mold your own quality/service philosophy—one that takes the best attributes of each and fits them together to create the ideal model for your organization. That's exactly how we built our approach to quality at Rosenbluth, and we have discovered that it works beautifully.

Our eclectic approach to quality has enabled us to understand and utilize statistical process control but not be controlled by it. One very important thing we've learned is not to let process stand in the way of progress. A key element in our approach to quality is common sense.

Extensive Research in the Quality Lab
Doing Your Homework to Make a Quality Choice

After a very humbling experience we began to see quality in a whole new light. For years our company has applied quality principles. We've long maintained the highest accuracy rating in our industry. Our clients were pleased with our service. So we assumed we were a "quality" company. We were in for a surprise.

When Motorola, one of our new clients, was awarded the prestigious Malcolm Baldrige Award for quality, it encouraged its suppliers to pursue total quality management and apply for the award as well. We got an application and intended to apply immediately. When we took a look at the application we were put in our place.

For those of you who might not have had the pleasure of reading this application, it calls for statistical measurement of just about everything a company does. It looks for every person in the organization to be utilizing these measurements as tools for continuous improvement. A history of consistent improvement must be proven statistically.

This was quality of a different species. We knew we operated on the principles of quality but we didn't have the tools to prove it, the same tools that help a company to improve. We had some decisions to make about what type of program we wanted. We thought that our level of quality deserved measurement. Continuous improvement was one of our most important goals. So we went for it.

The first thing we did was to study the quality processes of our clients, and the research of the complete lineup of quality gurus. We developed a pretty good idea of what we wanted out of a quality program and a clear understanding that we couldn't do it ourselves. So after an exhaustive search, we hired a total quality management consultant.

We selected the consultant not just based on his or her knowledge of statistics, although that's essential. It was important to find someone who would make the material interesting and understandable so we would all be enthusiastic about learning it and we would be able to apply it on a day-to-day basis. Because for most of us, sophisticated applied statistics seemed beyond our grasp.

With our partner in place and sights aimed high, we were ready to convert to total quality management. Quality was about to become serious stuff at our company.

Building a Quality Program
Where to Begin

We decided that a serious approach to quality would demand dedicated resources. We created a small department to analyze the company's quality needs, to develop training and implementation programs, and to continually evaluate our progress. This team ensures that all of our quality programs work together toward the results we want to achieve as a company. We create new and more demanding goals and they help us measure our way to success.

We built this team from inside our organization. Rather than hire quality experts and teach them about our company, we hired people who live the company and trained them to be experts in quality. In addition to our vice president of quality we have eight full-time trainers and specialists and five part-time trainers who hold positions within the company ranging from client services to accounting to reservations.

Our quality team completed rigorous training on quality principles and tools. Then they went into a week-and-a-half-long course to prepare and certify them to teach their fellow associates throughout the company.

In the first year of quality training, 42 percent of our associates completed the program—well over one thousand people. During the second year, the entire organization was trained. As new associates join the company, they complete the program within their first few months of employment. Our goal is to make quality an integral part of our lives.

The courses are tough, the material complex, and the investment significant, so we thought it would be important to recognize those associates who completed the training. Each person who graduates from our quality program receives a certificate and a pen with our quality logo. Associates who have just completed quality training return to their "natural work teams" (made up of the associates they work with daily), where they utilize the tools they have just learned. Natural work teams meet regularly—normally every two weeks. This gives the material immediate application and keeps the skills fresh.

Though our quality program is still in its infancy, our people take quality very seriously. On any given day, it's not unusual to walk into an office and find someone analyzing Pareto charts and cause-effect diagrams, discussing critical path methodology or another quality principle or tool.

Current processes are being studied by teams across the company, all putting quality tools to work. Human resources is working on reducing the cycle time on résumés. Accounting is reviewing their cash receipts procedure. Our industry relations group is studying the negotiating process with our suppliers. Individual offices or departments create "Focus of the Month" programs, concentrating on a particular aspect of service upon which they would like to improve. Our quality programs run the gamut from scientific to fun, all with intensity of purpose and measurable results.

To be effective, quality must permeate an organization. It's equally important for us to measure internal service as well as external. We need to see our human resources department using statistical process control to measure satisfaction, our ticket delivery people charting progress in on-time deliveries, and our receptionists tracking telephone hold time. The purpose is for quality to help us serve our internal and external clients and never to stop improving.

A Serendipitous Quality Experience
An Incentive Program with Unexpected Benefits

True quality actually costs *less* to deliver. We developed a program to improve our quality in the reservation process as a service enhancement to our clients. We were prepared to absorb the costs of the program, but we were pleasantly surprised to find that our costs were actually *reduced.*

We call our program "Pay for Quality," and it was designed to do what its name would suggest. It's an incentive plan for our reservationists based upon accuracy, professionalism, and productivity.

Unlike most incentive plans, which are based on quantity, our primary objective is quality. So accuracy is the first criterion. The performance matrix is built upon 100 percent accuracy. Incentive bonuses cannot be earned on reservations containing any errors.

The next criterion is professionalism. All error-free reservations can earn points for using elegant language, referring to the caller by name, confirming all information, offering additional services, teamwork, and other displays of professionalism.

The final criterion is productivity. The first two criteria must be met before quantity even becomes an issue. Only then does quantity play a role in the program. Obviously, the more quality reservations a person takes, the more points he or she will be able to earn toward a "Pay for Quality" bonus.

Though we believe that quality and quantity are not mutually exclusive, we expected that each reservation would take a bit longer. We anticipated that while quality would rise, productivity might fall slightly. And to add to that cost, we would be paying out substantial incentive sums to our people for achieving this level of quality.

The results were astonishing. Obviously, quality was enhanced, but the real surprise came when we saw productivity rising at the same time. People liked the challenge and specific objectives and they met them head-on.

We don't wait for reports to tell our people how they're doing. We monitor the service in progress, and provide immediate feedback to each reservationist. They are coached on the spot, while the transactions are still fresh in their minds, which allows them to use what they have learned on the very next transaction.

We expected that by the time we paid the incentives we'd be in the hole. But we were pleased to have met our goal of enhancing service. We thought the icing on the cake was the productivity gains we realized.

It didn't end there. The bottom line revealed the ultimate testimony to quality. Our people saw a 32 percent average gain in compensation, some as high as 77 percent. And productivity actually rose in the process. But we were shocked to learn that the company's operating costs were reduced by 4 percent because we were doing things right the first time.

We hadn't anticipated how much we were spending in checking and rechecking tickets, correcting errors, and shoring up quality on the customer service end. We caught the errors before the tickets left the door, but at a higher cost than we realized. Rework drives down productivity, and checkers, recheckers, and correctors cost money.

Turnover was reduced because people made more money and liked being able to determine their own salaries. The associated human resources and training costs plummeted as well. The final punch is that as corporations learned of our program to pay our reservationists based upon the quality of their service, our business increased significantly.

Everybody wins. Our clients receive the service they deserve. Our reservationists make more money and feel great about the service they provide. The company has lowered its operating costs, and those revenues can be reinvested in research, development, products, and programs for the future.

How Do You Know How You're Doing?
The Importance and Methods of Measuring Quality

Once these elements of our quality program were established, we determined measurable goals for quality improvement and set out to achieve our individual, department, and company goals. The key is to keep setting these goals higher and higher to keep our company moving forward. "Raise the bar," as high jumpers say.

We use internal and external barometers to measure our service. Internally, our company measures things like average speed of answering the phone, percentage of accuracy in obtaining the lowest fares, phone hold time, on-time delivery of tickets, and so on. Each department has its own services to gauge. We use measurement as a tool for further improvement.

An important component of our quality program is our associates' access to the tools that make it possible for them to measure their performance. It's not just management that's involved in continuous improvement. Each associate takes personal responsibility for the company's performance.

What about our clients? We keep a close watch on their

perception of our service through a variety of tools. We hold client focus groups and account reviews. We randomly enclose business reply cards with our clients' travel documents, asking for honest evaluation of our service. The feedback is disseminated to the appropriate departments for action, follow-up, and future planning.

When people are sitting in an airport or on an airplane they usually find themselves with time on their hands. That helps us get a good response rate. But it's not the number of replies that counts. It's what you do with them.

Our surveys also call for input on how our suppliers— airlines, hotels, and car rental companies—serve our clients. We share this information with our suppliers and we follow up with our clients on the results.

In addition to the business reply cards, we have a department that calls travelers on a random basis following their trip. We ask how everything went on that particular trip, how our service is in general, and how we can improve.

Our newsletter for our clients contains a business reply card with each issue. This survey includes specific questions about certain aspects of our service as well as general questions. We follow up on every comment.

Many of our clients have total quality management initiatives. This gives us the opportunity to utilize quality tools together to monitor service. We fax our charts and graphs to them and hold joint meetings to discuss our progress.

Every account has an account executive, whether it is a fully dedicated national account manager for one account, an account executive who works with a number of accounts, or a supervisor of an account-specific reservations desk who also serves as the account executive for that particular account. Each account knows whom to turn to with a concern or request. Our aim is to be proactive enough to anticipate our clients' needs before they materialize. Our clients should never tell us something we didn't already know about our service or their perception of it. But in reality, this is next to impossible, so we put quality tools to work to help us.

We also seek the evaluations of third-party audits. We carefully measure our service and accuracy levels, but when outside parties evaluate our performance it assures impartiality and objectivity. In fact, we encourage our clients to use these companies to reconfirm that they have made the right choice in selecting us to serve them.

Service Is Not an Advertisement
Guaranteeing Service

To many, service is an advertisement—cleverly crafted words that claim excellence in service. But service has to be a life-style. Companies that are serious about service should put their money where their mouth is. A few years ago we decided to do it.

Research told us we had the highest accuracy rate in our industry—consistently over 99 percent. We were pretty sure that rate would hold its own in any industry, anywhere.

We wanted our clients to know it. We wanted to show our associates how proud we were of their hard work and level of success, and we wanted to give them the chance to proclaim it to the world. So we created a program to guarantee our service.

I announced the program at our company-wide meeting and I must admit I was nervous to make the announcement. I was afraid their initial reaction might be apprehension. I thought we might hear a lot of mumbling like, "This really puts the pressure on," or "Does this mean that if I make a mistake I'll have to pay for it?"

The intent was certainly not to add pressure to our people's lives. And their accuracy rate was so spectacular it would have been unfair to ask them to pay for the very few errors they do make. Our goal for the program was to encourage our clients to look closely at the work our people were doing because we were so proud of it.

The reaction shouldn't have surprised me, but it did. When I announced that we would return the commissions earned on any travel arrangements we made incorrectly— in effect, working for free whenever we make a mistake— the room erupted into thunderous cheering. Our people knew they had something to be really proud of, and they welcomed the opportunity to rise to the occasion.

Service guarantees force companies to look closely at their accuracy rates and influence their clients to do the same. It's a great way to keep yourself on track. It's better to spend money refunding clients when they aren't satisfied than to forfeit money in lost accounts for the same reason.

Aspiring to Perfection
99 Percent Sounds Good, but We Have to Keep Trying

No company will ever be perfect, but the bottom line is that even the smallest mistakes aren't acceptable. This is a beast we all have to struggle with. And the service sector presents probably the most difficult terrain because of the perishability of the product a service company offers. You can't just return a vacation experience to a manufacturing plant to be repaired. Once it has been defective, that service is over forever—consumed instantly, to the lasting dissatisfaction of the consumer.

Not only are they perishable; services are personal—they actively involve people. They affect lives. If a service company had an error rate of 1 percent, that would be considered very good, translating to 99-percent accuracy or only one error per every one hundred transactions. Most companies would be proud of that.

Let's relate that to another scenario. If a surgeon has a 99-percent accuracy rating and operates on two hundred patients per year, in life-and-death situations, that means two people will die because of his 1-percent error factor.

Do you suppose their families will kindly appreciate the fact that he has an accuracy rating of 99 percent? Of course not, and the same goes for any other service. Who wants to be the person on the receiving end of the error? Any alternative to total client satisfaction is unacceptable.

Dealing with the Realm of the Possible
Reconciling with an Unattainable Dream

I once learned something in a grade school math class that parallels service. It's an illustration of infinity: If you stand any given distance from a wall and proceed half the distance, and then half the remaining distance, and then half again, you will never finally cross the room.

In service, there will always be room for improvement. Even if you manage to get all the basics right, there are literally infinite enhancements you could place on a service experience to make it that much better. That's one of our favorite aspects of being a service company. What would we do once we reached the wall anyway?

There Is Always Room for Improvement in Service

A *Summary*

- Examine your service as an attitude, an art, and a process. Attitude starts with the right people in the right environment. Art is important because some of the most memorable aspects of service are creative ones. Process brings order to service so people can concentrate on the added touches that bring it to life.

- Make sure you maintain an environment in which people feel encouraged to reach for the exceptional. They won't if they fear the repercussions of failure.

- Check for potential applications of the "busied-in" theory in your company. It's the same principle that a rowing team works on—distributing the burden among the many, not the few.

- Recognize your service heroes. Look for those who add special touches—don't let them go unnoticed. Frances Russell put a touch of caring in her service that went a long way.

- To build your own quality program, start by studying the many quality "gurus" as well as your clients, companies admired for their quality, and even your competitors. A cafeteria approach can be effective in determining the right program for your particular needs.

- A total quality management initiative takes commitment of time and resources—both human and financial. But it's well worth the investment. It costs less to do it right the first time. Consider working with a professional who can make statistics fun.

- Create a quality/service unit within your organization, whether it is a department or a task force, and charge this team with developing a plan to improve quality. Training in the use of quality tools will be essential.

- Consider a program in which your company pays based upon quality. Through ours, we proved that quality and quantity are *not* mutually exclusive. In fact, they are interdependent. Such a program is reassuring to clients and will also help your sales effort. Whether you're in the service industry or not, service is the key to every business.

- Set measurable quality and service goals for your company and keep raising them. Measure your progress both internally and externally.

- Consider guaranteeing your service. It's reassuring to your clients and motivating to your people. It will cost less to refund an unhappy client than to lose his or her business.

- Never be satisfied with the service you provide. Never feel you have finally "reached the wall," because if you do, there's nowhere to go but backward.

CHAPTER 9

THE CREATION OF A
A CULTURE

The great law of culture is: Let each become all that
he was created capable of being.

—THOMAS CARLYLE (1795–1881)

Most organizations are steeped in culture, whether positive, negative, or nondescript—even a seeming lack of
culture is a culture, in and of itself. The best way to describe
ours is one in which our people feel protected and embraced
by the company. But it wasn't always that way.

When I joined the company, I would have described
the culture as one that demonstrated the highest concern
for its clients, integrity, and tradition. The culture was
certainly admirable, but a stark difference from what it is
now. And it was largely the transformation of that culture
that brought us to where we are today.

We engineered a concerted change that puts our *people*
at the forefront. And there's been a surprising level of
interest from the outside in the forming of that culture. A
number of our clients, as well as nonclient companies, have

requested "cultural change" training from us. They've spent time in our offices talking with our people and studying our environment. They've talked with us about the steps we took in building the culture we have today.

First, we sought the input of our people, because they "live" the culture. We spent a lot of time in those early days daydreaming, as a group. We didn't know the technical terminology for the way we wanted to be, but we came up with a plan all the same. Looking back, it was probably better that way. We didn't mold our culture on principles we were *supposed* to buy into, but on those we naturally bought into.

For example, I don't think any of us had ever heard of the "inverted pyramid" style of management, but we knew we needed to support our people on the front line. We understood that their input was key because they were the ones closest to the client on a day-to-day basis. They were the ones "in the know."

We were much smaller then, but we knew we were building something special. We wanted to find a way to preserve it as we grew. Growth seemed certain. Our clients began telling us they wanted us to provide them with service nationwide. Word spread from client to client, and we began to receive requests to consolidate national travel accounts.

They told us they looked forward to talking with our people because they were happy and took pride in their work. They said our people showed a sense of ownership in the company. Our people had a "buck stops with me" attitude, and our clients liked the results.

This presented us with an enormous challenge because our culture wasn't formalized. As we grew rapidly from a regional to a national company and scores of new people joined our organization, how would we preserve what our clients had come to trust?

Live the Spirit
The Capturing of a Culture

No longer could we rely upon our culture to take root naturally, in new locations and in new associates. It was time to formalize our culture. We even gave it a name, as I've already mentioned: "Live the Spirit."

The first step was to capture what we had built, and put it into words that could be shared universally. We created a mission statement and an official set of philosophies and values. We even coined our own service language: "elegant language." This language is part of our overall service approach, which we call "elegant service."

The principle behind elegant service is to create a service experience far beyond that which is expected. We all know it when we experience it. Elegance by its very definition means refined, polished, graceful. Likewise, we strive to offer elegance in service that means those same things to our clients when they work with our people.

Elegant language is a way of speaking that truly reflects the way we feel about ourselves, our clients, and what we're doing. It's easy to slip into a lazy way of speaking that, when you stop to think about it, doesn't say what we mean nearly as well as do more expressive words.

Answering the phone "Hello?" doesn't say anything. People taking pride in themselves and their work would want to identify themselves and offer to help the caller. A better greeting would be, "Thank you for calling Rosenbluth. This is Hal Rosenbluth. How may I help you?" It takes a little longer. It takes a little more effort. But it means a great deal more to both the caller and the person answering.

The closing you would expect from most calls is "Goodbye." How inexpressive. How final. How uninspiring. This closing leaves both caller and answerer empty. Doesn't the following say it much better? "Thank you for calling Rosenbluth. It has been my pleasure to assist you."

We never refer to our people as "employees." If you look in a thesaurus, you'll find listed such harsh and demeaning words as "hireling," "servant," and "subordinate." These words far from reflect the way we regard our people. We refer to our people as "associates," which the thesaurus describes as "colleague," "partner," and "friend."

Once one is shown the benefits of expressing one's self in a more elegant, more meaningful manner, there's no turning back. But it's not just language; it's attitude. Our people have to feel it on their own. That's what gives meaning to the words.

Pentimento
True Colors Will Shine Through

There's a phenomenon in art called pentimento. It occurs when an artist paints on a canvas and then "erases" the image by painting over it. Years later, the original image begins to shine through. So pentimento is the reappearance of the original image through the new painting.

For example, if an artist painted a bowl of fruit and decided he didn't like it, he might paint it over in black and then paint a scene of a garden. As time elapsed, the bowl of fruit would begin to appear in the garden.

People's true colors shine through, and so do companies'. It's not enough for our people merely to answer the phone with the right words. Most faceless corporations train their people who spend time on the phone to use special language. A lot of companies have stopped calling people "employees." What makes it work?

What is called a sincere work is one that is endowed with enough strength to give reality to an illusion.

—MAX JACOB (1876–1944)

It's easy to provide helpful words but no help. What makes elegant language meaningful is that the people using it are ready to back it up with action. The words and the attitude with which they are spoken make our clients feel special, pampered. The service that goes along with those words is what makes them matter. To instill confidence in our clients that we are qualified to serve them, our people need to possess good communication skills, be positive, use proper grammar and vocabulary, and have thorough knowledge of our products and services.

But it's more than that. Our people must understand our clients—be able to put themselves in their shoes, know their policies, needs, and wants. It's important for each client to feel like he or she is our only client. And we need to perform accordingly.

What makes the term "associate" significant is that our people are treated with respect and care, hour after hour, day in, day out. A person's attitude about his company is a direct reflection of the experiences he has within that organization.

It's the depth behind the demeanor that counts. That

depth comes from the individuals who make up the organization and the organization's commitment to them. There's no faking it. The real state of a company will shine through in its daily interactions with its clients.

Reputations are not destinations, they are journeys. Each and every encounter between a company's people and its clients holds the power to enhance or diminish the company's standing.

What's the Bottom Line?
Our Answer to a Frequently Asked Question

We've been asked repeatedly what type of financial incentives we must be offering in order to get our people to care the way they do. The answer is that for the most part, that's not at all how we do it.

I asked our director of human resources what our people tell her about what motivates them and why they feel committed to this company. She said people tell her they look forward to coming to work in the morning. They don't tremble at how they're going to be treated or lie awake at night worrying. A lot of people in other companies live in fear over their jobs.

Our people tell her they feel happy and comfortable, and that kind of peace of mind holds a great deal of value for many people. It's not financial rewards that leave an indelible impression on people's behavior. It's the quality of life.

Spreading the Word
Communicating a Culture

None of the formalized elements of our culture are forced upon our people. We didn't invent them. We just looked around and saw what people were doing best and made sure everyone had the benefit of knowing what those things were.

A team of five associates visited all of our offices and observed people at work. They defined the elements of our service that made us the way we were. And we met with the top training executive of Ritz-Carlton hotels, because we greatly admired their style of service and sought to learn from it.

We then put together communication programs to clarify our approach to service and share it with everyone who makes it happen. For example, elegant language was already being used by most of our people. But to make sure that the people who joined the company understood the concept and took pride in it, we made display cards for each person to keep on his or her desk with examples of elegant phrases. Everyone really seemed to enjoy it. A number of associates have taken the cards home to their families, who liked what they heard when they called our offices.

There were laminated wallet cards with our mission statement and philosophies and values; daily computer briefings; and follow-up training programs to ensure a unified message. To kick it all off, we introduced our newly coined culture at a company-wide meeting. Anything this important calls for a face-to-face gathering of everyone.

Now our culture is firmly ingrained and is reinforced through a number of ongoing programs and publications created by our internal communications department. It's a never-ending process. But our most valuable tool is the protectiveness our associates feel about our culture. They guard it ferociously.

One Face
Keeping Culture Sincere

The root of the word *sincere* is a fascinating one. It comes from the Latin *sine* (meaning "without") and *cera* (which means "wax"). In the days of the Roman Empire, to possess marble was a sign of wealth and prestige and the smoother the marble, the more value it held.

Vendors in the marketplace would fill cracks in their marble with wax to make it appear flawless. But when the new owner returned home, the wax would melt in the heat of summer and the marble's true form would be revealed. Thus, the word *sincere* is derived from the term "without wax." After all, the cracks are what make marble so beautiful.

A key to making culture work is sincerity. We place the same emphasis on "Living the Spirit" with each other that we do with our clients. Our phone system enables each of us to know whether an incoming call is internal or external, yet we answer the same way each and every time the phone rings.

I think everyone finds it disconcerting to hear someone speak courteously to a client and then "switch off" the charm when speaking with a colleague. Demeanor has to be consistent to be sincere. People should treat each other like clients. What we should all strive for is the absolute antithesis of the Jekyll-Hyde complex.

The code of ethics has to be as strong as the work ethic.

Happiness in the workplace has to be recreated day after day. In our company, we have an unwritten code of ethics that says we'll never let each other down. We believe that if we accomplish that, we'll never let our clients down. If our sales team was to tell a client that we had a technology product that we didn't really have, they would let down their associates in technology, who would then have to attempt to make the product a reality in an unrealistic time frame.

How dependable a company's people are with each other is a good measurement of how dependable they are for their clients. Ultimately, in the example above, the client would be let down. Who's to say it's even possible to develop the product in the promised time frame? Furthermore, a product developed in haste wouldn't be as effective as one that was carefully planned.

We believe that when associates let each other down, they negatively affect each other's lives. And when they've done that they've overstepped their bounds. Around here, an associate who places another in a compromising position has signed his or her own ticket out of the company.

Corporate Salmon
The Selection of a Company Mascot

I shall be telling this with a sigh
Somewhere ages and ages hence:
Two roads diverged in a wood, and I—
I took the one less traveled by,
And that has made all the difference.

—ROBERT FROST, "The Road Not Taken"

Our company thrives on being atypical. We like to be different, to blaze new trails, stir up commotion. Our heroes are those who have dared to do things differently. If the stream is flowing one way, we're almost sure we should be swimming another. There have been times that by doing this, we think we may have actually changed the tide.

Because we're a group of contrarians who always insist on swimming against the tide, we selected the salmon as our corporate mascot. Our people love having a mascot. It's a great morale booster and team builder. And they particularly like the salmon.

I've received salmon of so many varieties since the adoption of our mascot. Associates, clients, and suppliers from across the country have sent some very unusual varieties. I have a statue of a salmon on wheels in my office along with a bean-bag salmon, a chocolate salmon, and of course the salmon stuffed animal we designed and produced for our clients.

We know that those who journey down a different road may have a tougher trip. But along it they will experience things that those who travel the traditional paths might never see. And most important in business, they will get there first.

The outside pressures of the world and the climate of our industry conflict with the way we operate. But we're sticking to our guns because we think we have created a culture that withstands fads and trends. Above all, it offers happiness, which is the key to success.

It Has to Be Fun
Celebrating Success

I've always had the theory that we can usually measure how successful we are by how much fun we're having. Think about it—does anyone ever have fun while failing? Not normally. On the other hand, winning is fun and hard-fought victories are even more fun.

Just look at Disney. One of the most highly respected and successful companies in the world made "fun" a business, and is legendary for being a great place to work. For instance, the company opens its parks one evening each year for a holiday party for its employees (or, as they call them, "cast members") and their families. Management, all the way to the top, operates the parks that night.

To me, fun and success are so intertwined that I can't tell anymore which comes first. Are those who enjoy their work and have fun at it the successful ones? Or is it that those who happen to be successful seem to have all the fun? I'm not going to chance trying to figure this one out. My philosophy is just to do both. Guaranteed fun. Guaranteed success.

In Chapter 6, I took you through our innovation seminar and mentioned that during it, the class breaks into small groups to come up with creative uses for a typical household product. Those who teach it tell me that without fail, the group that laughs the hardest and makes the most noise always comes up with, by far, the most ideas.

When you have fun, it shows. Haven't you ever talked with anyone who had a talent for "smiling over the phone"? It's a pleasure doing business with people like that, and the finest organizations are full of them. It's something that can't be simulated.

In fact, we make having fun part of our official strategy. Seriously. Our company's vision of the future is called "Vision 200," because 1992 kicks off our second century of business. In formulating Vision 200 we narrowed our strategic goals to just ten. One of those ten goals is to "Enjoy the journey."

Salmon Happy
Recognition Programs

We learned from our friends at Federal Express about an internal recognition program they have which they call "Bravo Zulu." So we asked more about it and created one of our own centered around our company mascot, the salmon.

The program recognizes associates who go above and beyond to help one another and our clients. We wanted the program to be alive on a day-to-day basis, so we created salmon materials our associates can use to recognize each other. For example, when we receive a letter complimenting an associate, the associate's leader sends him or her a copy with a salmon sticker on it. And associates send each other salmon note cards with messages of thanks or encouragement.

The highest honor in our company is the salmon pin. We also have service pins to recognize length of service, but the salmon pin is reserved for associates who far exceed even a salmon's expectations.

August Is for Associates
An Annual Event to Recognize Your People

It's important to take time all year to recognize the contributions of our people, but we all get busy and time seems to slip away. But we don't forget in August. That's "Associate Appreciation Month" at our company, a time set aside for special events and activities to thank our people.

Something special happens every day of the month. We encourage our suppliers to each sponsor a day, hosting a breakfast or a lunch for our associates. Every office has its own celebration.

Usually the events center around getting to know and appreciate each other better. For example, we'll have a contest to match people with their favorite story about themselves. It's a great way to get to know more about people you *think* you know.

One of our directors hitchhiked across the Sahara Desert and still holds his college's javelin record to this day. Another associate appeared with John F. Kennedy in a publicity photo, as an infant. Someone had a brown belt in karate and another was the recipient of the Eagle Scout Award. One person who's been with the company fifteen years was a child actress who starred in dozens of TV commercials.

Then there were the calamity stories, like the one from a vice president who, as a child, was driving across the country with her family. They drove off and left her at a gas station and didn't notice for several miles. Another associate slid down a wooden bannister at her high school when the football team won a championship. She got over one hundred splinters.

Our accuracy rating on matching the people with their stories is usually fairly low. There's so much we don't get to know about each other during the course of a workday, but these stories are part of our lives. They make us interesting people. They helped make us who we are.

We always end Associate Appreciation Month with our leaders sending a personal note to each of their associates, thanking them for their efforts and contributions. It all takes a little time, but our people really look forward to it each year.

Face to Face
Company-wide Meetings Boost Morale

When we celebrated our culture at that first company-wide meeting, we found it to be such a good investment that we have held one every other year since. The meeting is educational, motivational, productive, and most important, enjoyable. Because after all, it has to be fun.

It's the best morale booster we know of. Somehow bringing everyone together from all lines of business, departments, and regions creates a magic that's hard to duplicate.

The meeting takes place over a weekend, and we bring our people in from everywhere. There are educational seminars and social events. We host a trade show at which every department exhibits, to help associates chart their career paths. We invite clients and suppliers to speak to our people. We talk a lot about the future and what it holds, to make sure we're all headed in the same direction. It's a great forum for communication. It's a program we can't recommend highly enough.

Service Day

A Simultaneous Celebration of Service

We look forward to our company-wide meeting every other year, but in 1989 we had the experience of a lifetime. Tom Peters named Rosenbluth "Service Company of the Year." We were speechless (for about a week).

Then we decided to celebrate. We planned a company-wide celebration that would occur simultaneously across the nation. I hopped in a small charter and visited as many offices as I physically could in one day, from Allentown to Wilmington to Philadelphia, Rochester, Albany, and more.

There were four of us traveling from city to city in a very small plane. The day turned out to be one of the stormiest I can recall. Up in the air, thunder was rolling and lightning striking all around us. None of us was positive we would survive. There were at least forty white knuckles in that plane—probably more, but I was afraid to look in the cockpit to find out.

Then all of a sudden, out of nowhere, the storm lifted and we flew into a stretch of sun-streaked, billowing clouds. One in the group said, "Are we safe or is this heaven?" That was the joke for the day, but actually that day was a bit like heaven.

It was not only one of the best days of my career, it was one of the best in our company's history. What better occasion to celebrate than the occasion to serve our clients.

Ensuring Happiness in the Workplace
A *Summary*

- Every organization has a culture: Is yours the one you want? If not, change it. Seek input from your people. After all, they will be living the culture.

- Formalize your culture. Capture it. Name it. Make sure it withstands growth and change. Have organized programs to reinforce it—for example, a company-wide meeting. If your size prohibits a company-wide meeting, then consider programs that bring together as many people as possible who do not normally have the chance to meet face to face.

- Try instituting your own form of "elegant language"—one that fits your company's personality. You'll feel the difference and so will your clients. Announce the program with plenty of fanfare and encourage your people to buy into it and have fun with it.

- Encourage your people to treat each other like clients. Service and professionalism must begin in the office and emanate outward to your clients. Look closely for any traces of the Jekyll-Hyde syndrome.

- Think about adopting a company mascot. If you had to choose one today, what would it be? What would you like it to become?

- Celebrating success is essential. Formalized recognition programs can be effective, as can setting aside a special time each year to thank your people.

CHAPTER 10

THE BIRTH AND NURTURING OF IDEAS

For every really bright idea any of us ever comes up with, we've had plenty of poor ones.

I once had a bad idea that actually cost me a job. When I was in college, I studied criminology and had an internship with the state department of corrections. I worked with inmates to help them pass the high school equivalency test prior to their release. In my spare time, I organized athletic programs for the inmates, and I really enjoyed it. I could see these activities were important to them, and that was rewarding.

One day I had a great idea, or so I thought: I would put together an "away" softball game against a team of inmates from another prison. Needless to say, the idea didn't fly with the administration. They decided I was too trusting to continue to be responsible for the inmates in these programs. There's a fine line between creativity and naïveté, and I'm not sure to this day whether it would have worked or not.

That was two decades and thousands of ideas ago. Some

ideas are worth pursuing and some are not. The important thing is to keep ideas flowing and to see failures as steps toward success.

The meaning of the word *idea* found in the dictionary is "that which exists in the mind, potentially or actually." The key words are *potential* and *actual*. Because we all know there's a world of difference between thinking about something and doing it.

Everybody has ideas, some better than others. But they live in people's minds. They need to be brought out, refined, tested, and implemented. Ideas are the lifeblood of a company. They weave the fabric of its future, but they're fragile.

Ideas come to the curious—those who ask, "What would improve our lives?" But ideas have to be nurtured and cultivated. The stifling of ideas starts when we're young and are told, "Just do it and don't ask why," or "That's just the way it is." Creativity and innovation aren't emphasized enough in our schools, homes, or professional lives, but people who seek these gifts can and will find them in the right environment.

Lure the Muses
Creating an Environment That Inspires Ideas

There's a group of four of us who get together periodically on Amtrak to develop new ideas. We started riding the "creativity train" by accident. One day our vice president of marketing, director of industry relations, director of corporate development, and I were on our way from Philadelphia to New York for a meeting.

On the train we started kicking some ideas around. We came up with at least a dozen that we plan to implement.

When we arrived in New York we hesitated to leave the train, because we accomplished more on the journey than we knew we could in the meeting.

We decided to hold train meetings to come up with new ideas. It sounds crazy, but something just happens when the group gets together in that setting, and we're taking advantage of it. It's not that odd when you think about it. The great masters of creativity each have their own style, so why can't we?

Ernest Hemingway wrote many of his classic works in the south of France and Cuba, in its former splendor. But some of his greatest works came out of Casa de Botín, a restaurant in Madrid that's still open today. He would sit in the cellar and create masterpieces while drinking wine. In fact it was there that he wrote much of *The Sun Also Rises* and he gives the restaurant a mention in the final scene.

When Claude Monet set out to create an impressionist painting of the Rouen cathedral, he wanted to capture it at all different times of day, so he set up a series of twenty-five canvases, side by side in a shop across the street from the beautiful structure. There he would view it through the window and paint it over the course of an entire day. At sunrise he would work on the first canvas, moving to the second canvas a short time later, then the next canvas and so on, until he carefully recreated the cathedral in each distinct light.

It took him nearly three years, but the result was twenty-five masterpieces, each of the cathedral from the same view, but all completely different. Most artists would paint one picture at a time, but not Monet. What an ingenious way to do it—the way that made sense to *him*.

For centuries, artists have surrounded themselves with

sources of personal inspiration and they've insisted on working the way they desire. The legendary muses work their best magic where they are not constrained.

Maintaining a creative, energetic, and caring environment in which to work enhances the spirit of innovation in people. Incorporating individuality into the workplace is essential. Just giving people the freedom to create is an important beginning.

It is said that Henry Ford once hired an efficiency expert to evaluate his company. The report was positive except for an observation of one employee. "It's that man down the corridor," he said. "Every time I go by his office he's just sitting there with his feet on his desk. He's wasting your money."

In reply, Ford said, "That man once had an idea that saved us millions of dollars. At the time, I believe his feet were planted right where they are now."

Brilliant ideas will spring forth only in a nonbureaucratic atmosphere. Nothing creative ever comes from a slow-moving organization that crushes the entrepreneurial spirit in its people.

Ideas must never be suppressed. They need to be championed. While their flow should be continuous, an organized call for ideas can spark people's thoughts and keep creative talents sharp.

Our company holds an "Idea Week" each June, in which every associate is encouraged to contribute ideas. People take it seriously—most people submit at least one. To manage the flow of ideas we follow a process, because it's important that every suggestion be taken seriously, acknowledged, and analyzed, whether or not it is acted upon.

During Idea Week, everyone shares their ideas with

their immediate supervisor, to discuss them. Following that, they meet together with their manager to look at the ideas from every angle. Next, they all meet with the manager's manager, and so on. Along the way, insight and experience shape and refine them. When ideas have been explored to their fullest, they reach me with an action plan.

Every idea is considered carefully, and each member of senior management is encouraged to champion the ideas they believe have the strongest application. The originator of an idea plays a key role in all phases of its implementation.

Some of our finest ideas have come from Idea Week, but more have come as a result of our "open door" style and continuous emphasis on creativity. Every working day should be an "idea day."

Four Disparate Origins
Tracing Innovation to Its Roots

When we hear a great idea, we say to ourselves, "Why didn't I think of that?" Some innovations come from great scientists, and others come from everyday people who asked a question and turned the answer into an invention.

Ideas can come from every imaginable source. We just need to train ourselves to recognize the opportunities around us. Studying the roots of good ideas can help us spot the potential for an innovation.

I chose four ideas from our company with very different origins, and I'll trace each to its inception. I'll talk in depth about the first in chapter 14, and I discussed the second idea in chapter 7, so we'll look only at how these two ideas came about. The final two call for more detail.

These are just a few of the springboards for ideas that surround us all: (1) social responsibility; (2) finding a way to do something better; (3) creating a solution to an existing problem; and (4) filling a need in the marketplace.

A Company with a Conscience
Origin #1: Innovating Through Social Responsibility

As you will learn in Chapter 14, our office in rural North Dakota was one of the most fruitful ideas in our company's history. The origin of that idea was a desire to make a difference—to do something socially responsible. In an effort to come to the aid of a small farm community devastated by drought, we located an office there. And in the process, we gained outstanding human resources situated in an ideal place to do business, where quality is high and operating costs are low.

Not all programs designed to help people will further a company in such tangible terms. But there's nothing wrong with looking for opportunities to make them mutually beneficial to your company. There's no better way to encourage the commitment to these projects on the part of associates, clients, and shareholders than to have them add value to your company. In fact, it only helps ensure the life of the programs.

The origin of our idea was just the desire to help, but the way we implemented it was what led us to our discoveries in rural America. If we'd made a financial contribution rather than opened a temporary office, we never would have learned that rural America is a fantastic place to do business.

To make our decision, we looked for a way to benefit both a community and our company. The idea started with a perspective that spanned beyond our own company or industry, but we brought that idea home to come up with the plan. The result was a *permanent* benefit to the people of that community, to Rosenbluth, and to other companies who have since followed our lead.

How Can We Do This Better?
Origin #2: Creating Through Self-Improvement

If we ask ourselves each day, "How can we do this better?" we are bound to find ways to improve. Whether large or small, these improvements can lead to discoveries. As I discussed in Chapter 7, our PRECISION software was the answer to the search for a way to improve upon our processes and our service to our customers.

To refresh your memory, PRECISION is a conditional-logic software that guides our reservationists through the steps of booking our clients' travel, incorporating both the individual's personal preferences and his or her company's travel policy.

A couple of our people were saying, "This process constitutes the majority of our day-to-day service to our clients. We have to be able to do it faster, more accurately." Their pursuit of an answer ultimately led to the development of a product that changed our company.

Systems can be designed to facilitate any process in any organization. We just need to ask ourselves what we'd like to improve upon, and the answer becomes our innovation.

Smoke Signals for a Need
Origin #3: Filling a Need in the Marketplace

My office is a revolving door. Everyone is encouraged to walk in and run suggestions by me. On a typical day, one of our reservationists brought an idea to me that immediately sparked my interest. An idea doesn't have to be a first for it to be good, it just has to make sense for your company. This one did for ours.

This associate has a number of friends who are hearing impaired, who shared with her their frustration over their difficulty in booking travel. Many airlines and hotels have telecommunications devices for the deaf (TDD's), which enable the hearing impaired to communicate by telephone by typing what they want to say. The person on the other end does the same.

But one of the primary reasons most travelers utilize the services of a travel agency is to avoid the hassles of coordinating all of the components of travel. Why would anyone want to call seven airlines to compare prices and coordinate schedules when one call will do it and won't cost them any more? Our associate thought we should offer her hearing-impaired friends that option.

While she was still in my office to present the idea, I called together a task force comprised of people from operations, marketing, and technology. Within just a few weeks, we purchased TDD's, trained people to use them, and our Travel Department for the Deaf was created. The idea's originator was selected to head up the department.

We soon learned that several of our client corporations have hearing-impaired travelers who were relying on other people to plan their travel for them through our company. We probably would never have known that if the idea for the program had not been presented. Now those travelers can work directly with us.

We've also been contacted by organizations for the deaf and companies owned by hearing-impaired people who are interested in having us manage their travel. There was a need in the marketplace for these services. It makes you wonder how many other needs there are just waiting to be filled.

Creative Problem Solving

Origin #4: Developing a Solution to an Existing Problem

Years ago, we made a strategic decision that our growth would be client driven. Rather than pick a spot and hang an "Open for Business" sign, we'd grow when and where our clients required us to have a presence. This approach has served us well, but it presented its share of challenges along the way.

There are two primary challenges. First, there are certain locations where it's important for us to have an office, but with only a handful of people. These associates need to be able to take vacation and sick days, but even one person absent from an office that size can severely impact service.

The second major challenge is that clients often have an immediate need for us to be in a new market on short notice—for instance, when a client opens a new office in a city where we don't have one and they want local service. Or a company consolidates its travel and wants us to be in all of their major markets. Or perhaps it's a new client for us altogether, and we don't have an office in their headquarters city. Whatever the case, the demand for our services in a new location is often sudden.

Where do we find people who can fill in for the small yet important locations? Where do we find people who can "jump in" to assist where we've opened a new office, in which we've hired local people who are new to our company? The answer we came up with was what we call our "Mobile Reservations Team."

This idea came about during a strategy session in which we were discussing these very challenges. We began joking about taking some of our most experienced people in a mobile home across the country and stopping wherever they were needed. We carried the idea out to the edge of the envelope, picturing our people in "SWAT" team uniforms with mobile pagers and laptop computers. Soon, we modified the story to a team of professionals, ready to go on a moment's notice, not by caravan but by plane, and not in uniforms but normal business attire.

The crazy idea became a very viable answer to some very real challenges, and the Mobile Reservations Team was born. Over the past several years, they have worked in offices across the country, helping to establish new locations and filling in wherever needed.

Today, we usually shift business electronically to where the people are rather than send people to where the work is. But the Mobile Reservations Team was critical in seeing us through a period of rapid growth during a time when we didn't have the technology we have today.

Some ideas will have a limited life, but can still have significant value. That makes it all the more important to act quickly on your ideas. From joking about a travel SWAT team that day, we created a solution to an existing problem and laid the groundwork for the way we do business today:

If you can bring the people to the work, you can bring the work to the people. You never know where your next idea will come from.

How Many Paths Do You Let Yourself Cross?
A Broad Approach to Idea Generating

It seems that well-rounded people not only get more out of life, they contribute more to it as well. The broader your horizons, the broader your scope of understanding, and ultimately, the areas in which you can make a difference. If you stay on only one road, you limit the possibility of crossing so many paths that could lead you elsewhere. This is true in both our personal and business lives.

That's one reason that we seek a wide variety of people to join our company. And well-roundedness is encouraged throughout their careers with us. To come up with ideas, we try to look not just at what's happening inside our industry, but what's happening all around us.

A wider focus helps a company to spot trends early and to discover emerging needs in the marketplace. This might present opportunities to diversify. Or it can lead to a larger share of a company's current market, through gaining a clearer understanding of the pressures potential clients face and developing ways to ease those pressures.

Protect Them, but Not Blindly
The Importance of Germinating Ideas

Ideas must be championed, but not blindly. There's a delicate balance between encouraging ideas and recognizing the ones that won't be productive. One of the best methods to evaluate and refine an idea is "germination." Every idea is like a seed that needs to be cultivated, but the plant has to be strong to survive. Ideas need to be put to the test to see if they will work.

The best place to start is to objectively study each and every idea with the person(s) who suggested it, to ensure that it can and will work, and to determine whether or not it should be modified or even expanded. In an open, honest, and encouraging environment, this will be possible without people feeling threatened or defensive. A spirit of teamwork has to surround the building of ideas, because they become stronger with input from other people.

To test my own ideas, I like to "sprinkle" them around to associates in a variety of departments, regions, and levels within the company. I particularly like to run them by people I know will regard them with the least reverence. Their constructive criticism improves the ideas because we all have a natural tendency to be too personally involved with our own ideas to see them objectively. The more ideas are put to the test, the more powerful they become.

That's why I think "weekend thinking" is dangerous. Most truly dedicated people can't completely get their minds off work, even in their free time. Opportunities, problems, and solutions pop into their heads, and their natural reaction is to work through those thoughts and return to the office with solutions. The dedication is great, but creating solutions within our own limited boundaries narrows our ability to envision how the answers we've arrived at will play out. The solutions can have a ripple effect on the entire company.

People come back to work on Monday morning all fired up about the ideas they came up with over the weekend.

They set them in motion right away. But without input from other departments, their ideas can be redundant, counterproductive, even destructive. Ideas need to be shared to be enhanced. Otherwise we limit them to just our own creativity. We should seek to surround ourselves with imaginative people and help bring each other's ideas to fruition.

Besides, people need the outside stimulation that time away from work can bring. Louis Brandeis, associate justice of the U.S. Supreme Court from 1916 to 1939, once said, "I find that I can do a year's work in eleven months, but I can't do it in twelve."

Steps to Encouraging Ideas in a Company
A Summary

- Encouraging fresh ideas to spring forth from your people starts with the right environment—an energetic, creative, and caring environment from which you remove the fear of trying something new.

- Hold an "Idea Week" to encourage people to be thinking of new and better ways to do things. Innovation is an art that needs to be practiced. Every day should be an "idea day," but it helps to set aside an official time for ideas.

- Continually squelch bureaucracy in your company, because slow-moving organizations crush entrepreneurial spirit and stifle ideas.

- Recognize that ideas come from a variety of sources, such as the four outlined in this chapter: accepting social responsibility; finding a way to do something better; discovering a need in the marketplace; and finding a solution to an existing problem.

- Examine the origin of innovations, inside and outside your industry. Study the steps in developing successful ideas and recreate them.

- Never, ever allow an idea to be suppressed in your organization. People will come forth with idea after idea if they know their suggestions will be respected and acknowledged.

- If an idea is implemented, give plenty of credit and recognition to the originator of the idea and allow him or her to be involved in its implementation.

- Keep a wide focus, because you never know where your next innovation will come from. The best thing that can happen to an idea is for it to be shared with as many people as possible. Well thought-out ideas are the most powerful.

CHAPTER 11

THE GARDENING PROCESS

In the past few years, we've all become couch editors. In our hands is the power of remote control, and we use it like a weapon. Whenever we don't like what we see on TV, we just switch the channel. When a commercial comes on we cruise the stations, and if we don't find something we like, we mute the sound. When we rent a movie and it's moving slowly, we fast-forward to the parts we like. I've even found myself at live sporting events clicking my thumb in search of my remote, to fast-forward time-outs.

There are a lot of situations in life where remote control could come in handy. Most of us have people we'd like to mute. I'd like to fast-forward service and product development and to edit out mistakes the way you can with videotape. There's no remote control for that yet, so the best we can do is to develop processes to edit our organization to be the best for our clients, because they don't have a remote control for it either.

The selection process is a great start, but even the most thorough selection process isn't foolproof. Companies need

169

to make an ongoing effort to keep the right people and encourage those who aren't pulling their weight to move on. This might sound incompatible with our philosophy of putting our people first.

On the contrary. We owe it to our people to create an environment where they are surrounded by others who care as much as they do, and who work as hard—who have a positive attitude. And we owe it to our clients, too. Which client should we pick to be served by someone who doesn't measure up? We can't do that to any client and we won't.

We liken it to carefully tending a garden. In order for the crop to grow, the weeds need to be pruned away. It takes a sharp eye and a steady hand to weed the one without damaging the other. But it's a never-ending process that's essential.

Chutes and Ladders
Creating Clear Routes to Advancement and Demotion

As a child I was quite fond of the game Chutes and Ladders. I guess when some things hit home, they stay home. Even today, that game plays an invisible role in our company. Donald Trump might have Trump: The Game, but at Rosenbluth we live our own version of Chutes and Ladders. Here's how it works.

In the game, the objective is to work your way up the playing board until you reach the top. All players start at the bottom, and with the spin of a wheel determine how many spaces they may advance each turn. There are ladders on the game board which enable the player to advance rapidly. When players land on a space that intersects a ladder, they get to jump over spaces. Ladders are shortcuts to the top. On the other hand, players have just as much chance of landing on a chute, which sends them back to square one.

While we don't keep game boards in our offices, we certainly have chutes and ladders. But the fundamental difference is that the moves people make are completely of their own choice, not left to the spin of a wheel. What's more, everyone in our company knows just where the chutes and ladders are.

Figuratively speaking, every company has its form of chutes and ladders. The secret is to keep careful watch over how they're working. Are the right people being lifted to the top, or are all the wrong ones climbing their way up?

Recognition systems send loud messages to people and affect their behavior. People who advance become role models for others. We've found that frequent evaluation of what type of person is moving in which direction can be helpful in making sure the system encourages the right values.

In corporate America, people often perceive that the climb to the top requires stepping on others. Perhaps it does in some organizations. But in ours we make it an instant chute. We have a rule that no one progresses at someone else's expense.

Conversely, being discovered helping someone else in the company is an instant ladder. There is no faster way to rise to the top. Our people delight in seeing someone ascend a ladder, because it's a given that they deserve it. Usually it's the people they've helped along the way who make the noise that gets them recognized.

'Tis the Season
Watch People's Contributions So They Don't Have To

We have eschewed traditional management styles and created what we refer to as our "Santa Claus" style of management. Yes, you've got it—we know who's been naughty and who's been nice and we reward people accordingly. We do our best to eliminate politics by creating an environment in which it doesn't work. Customarily, people make power plays to catch the eye of those who can promote them. In our company, people know that all the grandstanding in the world won't get them as far as excelling at what they do and helping those around them shine.

It's a fun way to manage. Our leaders enjoy promoting those who truly deserve it yet do not expect it, as opposed to those who expect it and may or may not deserve it. But more important, it's an *effective* way to manage. People begin to spend more time *doing* their work and less time promoting it.

Unfortunately, politics exists in every organization, to a certain degree, and it's a tremendous time waster. Internal political efforts don't add value. In fact, they take time away from value-adding activities. If people are spending 25 percent of their time covering their tails, 25 percent documenting what they have done, and 25 percent figuring out how to get ahead, then all that's left is 25 percent. That's not enough. With profit margins as narrow as ours we need 100 percent.

People fear that without positioning, their efforts won't be noticed. It's up to the company to assure them they will. Most people are just behaving the way they've been conditioned to behave. We find they welcome the opportunity to drop the politics when they learn it's not necessary.

It normally takes a while before new associates learn to relax, cut back on the memos and backtracking, and begin to trust. But when they do, their productivity soars. If companies could reduce politics by even half, think of the gains in productivity they could achieve.

This management theory, in practice, is only as good as the leaders who carry it out. It's nothing more than propaganda if, in reality, the grandstander is the one who's promoted. To make it work, leaders have to walk the talk. One way to ensure it is to make it part of the performance appraisal system. Objective performance measurements will determine who's really working. Leaders have to actively seek those who are quietly contributing, by carefully evaluating actual work completed by each individual.

Our company has a policy that says a written performance appraisal with objective measures (which have been established up front) must be submitted before a merit increase can take effect. This helps ensure that those who are rewarded are deserving. Our performance appraisal system is job-description driven, and therefore highly personalized. Each job explanation includes specific accountabilities, predetermined measures for success, and time frames for completing those actions. Every position incorporates our culture, company goals, and teamwork.

Teamwork has to play an important part in the performance appraisal process. To ensure it, it must be measured and rewarded. We've found that the best way to find out who's helping others is by asking. It won't work to ask people how they've helped others. To find out the real story, people should be asked how they've *been* helped and by whom.

"Just Ask Why"
Question What You're Doing

Grown-ups never understand anything for themselves, and it is tiresome for children to be always and forever explaining things to them.

—Antoine de Saint-Exupéry, *The Little Prince*

Children have a delightful way of looking at things. They always bring questions to mind—things we haven't thought about in years. Every other word is "Why?" They take nothing for granted and make everything new. Somehow they cut through to the truth. They find the most direct route to where they want to go.

One of our vice presidents keeps a drawing in his office showing a soccer team trying to find out which goal is theirs as they prepare to drive down the field. He had it made because he never wanted to forget a lesson he learned from his son.

His son's first grade soccer team had a losing season and their coach asked them what would help them win. They told him they sometimes got confused about which goal was theirs. Something so simple, so easy to remedy, but so crucial to success. Their coach promised his team that the next season, he would stand on the sidelines and point the way to the goal throughout every game. Guess what—they were undefeated that season.

These are the kinds of lessons that might seem simplistic to an adult, but how many businesses get off track from their real goals? And how often are team members running in all different directions? We believe there's plenty we can learn from a childlike look around us.

We set out to capture that clear view of the world, that

special inquisitiveness, and make it work for our company, so in early 1990 we unveiled an internal campaign we called "Just Ask Why." It is designed to help us look for better ways of doing everything we do. The campaign continually points out that sometimes the best way to do something is not to do it at all.

Our team of top leaders attended Tom Peters's "Skunk Camp," a week-long program in which executives from a wide variety of companies discuss management issues and the landscape of the future. On a tip we learned there, we set up "time teams" to study how we could be more efficient. The teams are from all walks of the company, and the primary ground rule is that there are no protected areas. Everything is fair game and must be studied with complete objectivity.

The study of time and motion certainly isn't new. People have been fascinated with it for centuries. But while time and motion analysis is commonplace in the manufacturing sector, it is often ignored by service companies, much to their loss.

Our time teams scrutinize every procedure, process, and program to answer three burning questions: (1) "Why do we do this?" (2) "Do we need to do it at all?" (3) "If so, how can we do it better?"

To be effective, people can't be afraid of the answers. If people are doing things they don't need to do, then where is the fulfillment? They'd be better off doing something new that shapes the future of the company.

When we initiated the time-team concept we estimated we were spending 15 percent of our time doing things we didn't need to do, either because efforts were being duplicated or because we hadn't stepped back recently enough to take a look at why we were doing certain things at all.

The jury is still out on just how much time we have saved, but it looks like we will surpass our expectations. We found that not only were we using our time inefficiently, we were spending valuable time improving on those things we didn't need to be doing in the first place. This brings to my mind the image of a hamster on a running wheel.

There was a splendid article in the July/August 1990 issue of *Harvard Business Review* about the need to reengineer companies. It contained one passage that stuck in my mind: "At the heart of reengineering is the notion of discontinuous thinking—of recognizing and breaking away from the outdated rules and fundamental assumptions that underlie operations. Unless we change these rules, we are merely rearranging the deck chairs on the *Titanic.*"

A classic example of the deck chair allegory was our persistent use of something called "control cards." For years we kept a handwritten index card for each reservation made, which was used to follow all of the steps of the reservation process from the initial call to ticketing. But years ago, we discovered an enhancement in our computer system that tracked the same process for us. We decided that we didn't need the control cards and we'd stop using them. We thought we had stopped.

We were wrong. When our time teams dissected our reservations process as part of our "Just Ask Why" campaign, we discovered people were using the cards as a sort of security blanket. They were afraid to let go of the old system even though the new system rendered it obsolete. The final elimination of this process saved a significant amount of time, which was rerouted to productive activities that contribute to the bottom line. We found out we can't afford not to ask why.

Our time teams shook the organization. No longer did

we just do the same things we always did. We began at every turn to ask ourselves the three questions, and those questions and answers continue today. People have remarked that they find themselves carrying this same philosophy into their personal lives and making the most of their time—all of it.

But it's fundamental that we "just ask why" about ourselves as often as we "just ask why" about what we do. . . .

Vertical Interviewing
Question How You're Doing

When was the last time you asked the people you lead to honestly evaluate you? To make suggestions on how you might improve? We have a tool to help us do just that. We call it "vertical interviewing." It works from the bottom up, but it has to start at the top.

Vertical interviewing began at Rosenbluth Travel when at the end of a review with one of my vice presidents, I asked her to honestly evaluate me. I must admit, that day I was humbled. She told me a lot of things. One was that I didn't listen when I had a lot on my mind. And usually that's when it's most important for me to listen. That's when there's something going on in the company that's concerning me.

She went on to say that when I'm not listening, people read the wrong cues from me and it affects the decisions they make. The consequences of such a flaw could be disastrous. I found myself endlessly reviewing hypothetical situations in my mind, and it really bothered me.

So I asked our director of training to work with me to

improve my listening skills. We set up a program to meet once a month to evaluate my progress and to practice techniques that help me keep focused on the conversation at hand. One of the most helpful suggestions from these meetings has been to bring one meeting to a close before beginning another. He told me he had noticed that because I allowed no time in between meetings, my mind was often a meeting behind. I'm working on taking a few minutes to jot down thoughts or put plans into motion before tackling the next subject.

We still meet, and the feedback I've gotten from those around me is a great motivator. I think I still have a way to go, but it's a good feeling to know I'm improving.

After that initial experience, I was eager to have each of my vice presidents evaluate me, and today the process is spontaneous and ongoing. But at least once a year, I still hold a formal vertical interview with each person who reports directly to me.

This year, I added another step to the process—accountability. I took all the written reviews I received and read them aloud during a meeting with all who had reviewed me. I asked them to hold me accountable for improving in each of the suggested areas. I already feel the heat, and that's good.

Vertical interviewing is both difficult to do and to accept. At first, people were cautious. They'd only give me one or two suggestions, followed quickly by compliments. But with each vertical interview the constructive criticism increased. I don't think it's because I was losing ground. It's because people began to feel more comfortable with the process and secure that they could be frank.

Sure, the truth hurts, but it helps to hear it. You know you're open to self-improvement when you look at constructive criticism as a gift from a friend. In my case, it must be Christmas every day in my office.

Once our associates saw how effective vertical inter-viewing was, the process began to filter throughout the organization. Today, vice presidents are reviewed by direc-tors, who are reviewed by managers, who are reviewed by supervisors, and so on. It's a mutual process, both vertically and laterally.

Vertical interviewing is a good barometer of morale, leadership skill, and ultimately, client satisfaction. Every-one should be given the opportunity to participate in the process. To help ensure it, we formed quality assurance teams to travel to all of our offices to interview our people. They ask associates to evaluate their leaders, who are asked to evaluate their leaders and so on. This gives the vertical interviewing process a nudge and offers people an additional chance to say what's on their minds. It's also a great way to cross-pollinate ideas across the country.

The final part of the quality assurance process is to meet with clients to ask them to review us. The results are then shared with the associates who serve those clients and a plan is developed to implement the clients' suggestions. Follow-up calls are made to the associates and the clients, to ensure that the plans are being carried out and that they're effective. But even the best-laid plans have to be adaptable enough to withstand outside pressures.

Lipomanagement
A Process to Keep Lean

The downsizing of the late eighties and early nineties has been a crash course in learning how to operate a leaner organization. Management experts have been preaching for years that lean is the way to go, but it's easier said than done. No company wants to lay people off. Then it becomes a numbers game in which some really good people can come up short.

A more fair method is to keep a trim organization based upon merit. We've actually found that in an environment like ours, which squelches politics, a natural attrition occurs, and the best people stay. This is a different culture, and people who don't buy in generally wind up leaving. It's just a matter of time. Those who don't know how to operate without politics become frustrated. Those who aren't pulling their weight begin to feel out of place, surrounded by those who are.

Every company's goal is to keep the muscle and lose the fat. To achieve it, they can't be afraid to cut out nonproductive programs or people. They can't hesitate for a moment to make room for the muscle—programs that work, people who make things happen, people who care. "Fat" just makes a company move more slowly, and in today's competitive environment, who can afford that? It's a demotivator to those who make up the "muscle."

Natural attrition is helpful, but it's often not enough. Marginal performance will weight a company down. To be fair, it has to be made crystal clear, up front, that marginality is not condoned and that the company can't make room for it.

We compare it to preparing for a trip. Those who travel frequently have learned the secret: Pack lightly. Only neophytes drag half the things they own with them. They bring everything they might ever possibly need . . . just in case. Experienced travelers know they can find whatever they need when they arrive, if they have to. They don't burden themselves with what they *might* need. They bring what they *know* they need.

The same applies to companies. Fit organizations don't carry excess baggage. They keep a pure environment with their best people. They don't make room for those who are marginal, because it's not fair.

Leaders must be strong enough to give their people frequent and honest feedback. Those who are marginal need to know it and be encouraged to improve, because marginality is contagious. It discourages those who give their best and is a sure way for a company to be left behind.

Run from the Dinosaurs
Keep Moving as a Company

Two dinosaurs took a break from their lunch of tasty treetops to observe a caveman trying unsuccessfully to cart his belongings along in a crate resting upon square stone wheels. With every bumpy turn, the dinosaurs would hear a loud crash and his cart would tip over. They laughed uncontrollably and said, "We dinosaurs will rule the world forever." Unfortunately for our two friends, their analysis wasn't quite accurate, and they haven't been heard from for several thousand years.

For companies to avoid becoming dinosaurs, they need to keep things moving; stir up change. When people are given the opportunity to move around, complacency is replaced by energy. Change is exhilarating and it keeps people on their toes.

How appetizing would it be to eat the same thing for every meal, every day of the year, year after year? Not very. How inspired would the person be to prepare that same meal over and over? Not at all. Variety is the spice of life. We all crave it. We need to remember that in business.

To keep things fresh, once or twice a year we make major structural changes and reorganize regions, divisions, and departments. While our long-term goals remain the same, we take these opportunities to reevaluate our strategies. As a result, we've seen some very positive effects in terms of creativity and energy. But very often, these changes bring side benefits of their own.

For example, last year we combined our sales and client services organizations. This says to our clients that we're merging promises made in the sales process with performance in service. We're structured to make it happen. Our clients like the change and so do our people.

Our vice president of the combined effort says he sees our sales people as hunters and our client services people as farmers. They both put food on the table and we can't live without either one. The secret is for them to work together to provide our clients with all they need.

But we go a step beyond just changing the structure of the company. We also move individuals around the organization, throughout their careers. As a result, we've seen a new breed of leader emerge, one who is flexible and well rounded.

Dismantling Compartments
Encouraging Cohesiveness

Most companies have departments, of some sort. We have them too. The danger lies in the fact that departments easily become "*compartments*," each with its carefully drawn boundaries and closely guarded domain.

There are certain efficiencies that can be captured by the sharing of resources and procedures within various areas of specialization. But there is a natural tendency for those areas to metamorphose into territories when people become too busy to look beyond their own niche. Fresh ideas can't flow in this type of environment. When people and ideas are guarded, their growth is stunted. Conversely, ideas breed ideas and often, input from people "outside" our specific area brings a new perspective to things.

Departments may be a necessary evil, but the natural barriers they erect should be continually torn down. One way to do it is to base leaders' compensation largely on the company's performance as a whole. The bonus system for our leaders is weighted equally between individual and company performance. This puts emphasis on teamwork that extends beyond department or line of business.

Another method to decompartmentalize departments is to encourage the cross-utilization of resources—both human and capital.

The Cross-pollination Principle
Keep People Moving

Cross-pollination has brought us some of the most spectacular varieties of plants and flowers known to the world. It's an old science that perpetually creates new wonders. Its value is the strength that results from exposure to diversity. The same principle is true with people.

The more a person knows about a wide variety of subjects (or in the case of a company, a variety of departments), the more of an asset he or she is. And access to a variety of leaders strengthens people as well.

There is a theory in academia that a person reaches the scholastic pinnacle when subjects begin to relate to one another. When knowledge of biology makes a literary work clearer. When understanding of geometry enables one to appreciate a work of art. When erudition in geology begins to put events in history into perspective.

Cross-pollination facilitates well-roundedness and heightens teamwork to astounding levels. The more people know about the "big picture" and the company's goals and objectives, the more they will be empowered to contribute. One tool that can be helpful is focus groups. They aren't new, but they're a highly effective means of cross-pollination because they offer a full spectrum of viewpoints upon which to base decisions. Furthermore, they give the people involved a chance to "buy in" to the program or policy being developed.

Like it or not, people usually come to the table with their own agendas, which can bear on decisions that affect many. For example, let's say there's a company that operates an employee cafeteria in which those responsible for preparing the food are also responsible for selecting the menu. Chances are, they will prepare food that (1) fits their personal taste and/or (2) they find easy to prepare. There's a good chance the lunchtime crowd will choose to bypass the cafeteria and run for the border (Taco Bell).

The best decisions are made with input from as many people as possible. It's vital to include the widest possible cross-section of people in the development of processes, procedures, and products.

When we held focus groups around the country to assess our benefits program, we learned that our policy on "sick days" was not current with our people's needs today, in one very important aspect. Our former policy allowed for six paid days per year for personal illness. What we learned was that people needed days off for important family events more than they needed sick days. People need to take their children or parents to doctor's appointments or to attend parent-teacher conferences.

Our policy was changed so that people can stay healthy and use these days as they need them. We call it our "family responsibility program," and it supports our people for what's important in *their* lives. The plan is based on flexibility. Time may be used either in partial or full days and is taken at the discretion of the associate for illness, family obligations, or medical appointments.

Accordion-Style Management
Preparing Your Organization for External Pressure

All industries fall upon good and hard times. In our company's case, potential danger can be found in decreasing airfares and reduced corporate travel programs.

It costs exactly the same amount of money to book, produce, deliver, and track a $200 ticket as it does a $500 ticket, but our commission remains at the standard 10 percent of gross. Which means we can do the exact same work for $20 or $50. Lower fares mean lower revenues for the same amount of effort.

The squeezing of profits doesn't end there. Cutbacks in budget and personnel in corporations across America have affected us immensely. We manage the travel accounts of nearly two thousand corporations, and when times are hard for them, we share the burden. When budgets are slashed in cost-cutting measures, travel is one of the first discretionary expenditures to be cut. And when our clients make the choice to reduce their travel programs, we can suffer huge losses because we have assumed the resources to provide service for their original volumes.

Let's say Rosenbluth manages the $50 million travel account of a manufacturing company. We would have some eighty people dedicated to serving solely that account. Suddenly, the company faces financial pressures and cuts its travel expenditures in half. Do we let forty people go? No. Not if we can help it.

We don't subject our people to layoffs, downsizing, or cutbacks in personnel. We don't do it just to be nice. It's good business. We truly believe that creating a secure environment makes people more productive. Also, top talent won't jump ship when competitors attempt to lure them away in good times.

Do All Accordions Come with Monkeys?
The Trials of Flexibility and Steps to Success

Yes, all accordions do come with monkeys. In this case, the monkey on our back is the threat of the imminent squeeze after expansions. But our accordion-style management means maintaining a flexible organization that can expand quickly and effectively with the acquisition of a major account, and tighten its reins just as quickly and efficiently when times are lean. Businesses continually face growth and decline, but we think the secret is to avoid layoffs, cutbacks, and drastic downsizing. And we have developed a four-step plan to help us do it.

The first step in our accordion process is to fuel our sales effort in order to maintain the proper balance of productivity. We then redirect underutilized staff to serve those new accounts. You might be thinking, "Why don't they fuel their sales effort all of the time?" We do, but we plan our growth very carefully to ensure consistency without straining our resources.

Originally, we targeted the accelerated sales efforts to the particular region or city in which the squeeze took place. But one day, an interesting opportunity presented itself. The volume of an enormous account dropped dramatically in a cutback. Simultaneously, we acquired a major account in another city, where our presence was minimal.

We presented the idea to our new client to service their account out of another city, where we had an operation in place that ran like clockwork. The start-up costs had already been absorbed. The staff was already a team.

Our client was sold on the idea. And since that time, we haven't limited our "accordion" sales effort by location. With today's tele-linked society, we can provide service from any location. We simply move business to where our resources are.

The second step in the accordion process is a combination of promoting from within and eliminating unnecessary work. Ultimately, the goal is to identify positions that are not essential and move those resources to where they are needed, providing chance for advancement in the process.

As a fail-safe to detect wasted resources, our vice presidents routinely review hiring requests as a team. When a current position is vacated or a new one created, it is analyzed for its value to the company. If the position is justified, it must be filled from within if at all possible. This creates another opening, which is then evaluated for its contribution to the company, creating a cycle of objective evaluations of positions throughout the organization.

Through this process, we have discovered a significant

number of jobs that are not vital to the organization: positions that are draining resources from what's really important.

The third step is to cross-train our people, which enables them to shift from one position to another successfully. This is a hybrid between the cross-pollination principle and dismantling of compartments discussed earlier in this chapter.

A standard reaction during lean times might be for people to try to look busy in order to justify their existence. People need the opportunity and the security to seek new challenges. In our one-hundred-year history we have never had a layoff, so our people don't have to be afraid to say, "I'm not busy. Find something worthwhile for me to do."

This brings us to the fourth step: to instill confidence in our people that each will have a challenging, fulfilling, and enriching position in good times and in bad. It may not be the position they have today, but it will be a position that is vital to the company, because we don't have positions that are not.

The ultimate test of our accordion management theory came in 1991. The gulf war and the recession rendered it the worst year in our company's history. Travel came to a virtual standstill. Despite the layoffs initiated by our competitors, nobody at Rosenbluth lost his or her job. In the short run, our people benefited from remaining employed. In the long run, the company benefited by keeping the best people and cementing their loyalty.

But we couldn't have weathered the storm without the dedication of our people. First, our associates initiated a program they called "Operation Brain Storm," which generated over two hundred cost-saving ideas. The second action was a pay freeze (not a cut). Third, our top leaders took a voluntary pay cut which spurred the fourth move, in which associates from across the country took voluntary time off without pay. Through these four displays of support, we made it through in good shape.

Developing a Gardening Process
A Summary

- Make sure you have clear routes to advancement and demotion in your company that send the right messages to your people.

- Watch people's contributions so they don't have to spend their time measuring their worth and bringing it to your attention. Give"Santa Claus" management a try.

- Visibly reward those who help others—make it a requirement for promotions and see how your teamwork improves.

- Implement a "Just Ask Why" campaign to take a hard look at everything your company does and how it can be done better (or if it even needs to be done at all).

- Make "vertical interviewing" a practice in your organization. Offer the opportunity for everyone to evaluate the leadership that guides them. It also works laterally.

- Encourage leaders to make room for the muscle (programs that work, people who care) by eliminating fat (marginal performers).

- Keep people moving. Stir up change. It keeps them on their toes, develops cross-departmental understanding, breeds innovation and fresh ideas. Dare to rethink your structure every now and then.

- Discourage departments from becoming compartments by tying leaders' compensation to company performance as much as individual contribution.

- Encourage cross-pollination of people. Generalists better understand the "big picture"—the company's overall objectives.

- Create an "accordion" management plan that works for your company to enable you to shift resources and stretch or shrink for peaks and valleys in business.

CHAPTER 12

LOOK AROUND YOU

A few years ago we lost an $80 million account. It was devastating. We didn't see it coming. For years we served the account like a dream, and then all of a sudden our dreams were shattered.

Our associates who served that account were taken aback because they believed their service had been outstanding. In fact, the client agreed. But we lost the account nevertheless. You can never be prepared for a loss like that, but we should have at least seen it coming.

Our client was facing the toughest time in the company's history and decided to make a number of major changes. Their choice of a travel partner was one of them.

It seems everyone else recognized their troubles before we did. We were so busy concentrating on providing them with service, we didn't notice that our competitors were circling like sharks. Our service was great, but their highest priority was drastic cost cutting. It's like being all dressed up with no place to go.

We missed the opportunity to adapt our strategy to their

changing needs and it cost us dearly. We just didn't see the writing on the wall until it was too late. We'll never know if we could have saved the account with a new approach or not, but we regret not giving ourselves the chance to find out. The account was gone and it was our job to minimize damages.

The first thing we did was to immediately involve all of the people who were impacted by the loss. We met as a team—over 169 of us—and determined our strategy together. These were some of our best people, in whom we had invested a great deal. We wanted them to remain with the company, but they had to have a client.

In the meantime, we developed a transition plan so that our departing client's service would be uninterrupted by the change. We had served this account faithfully for years and we wanted to uphold our reputation for service. This kept our people who were dedicated to the account active while we pursued new accounts for them to work with.

We accelerated our sales effort and eventually we acquired new business. But what took place in the meantime was crucial to company morale. We kept a list of each of the 169 people affected, and our team of top leaders met every Monday morning to discuss the placement of each person, one by one.

It was critical that each individual be fully utilized in his or her new role. As a company, we couldn't afford just to find something for them to do. We operate on a tight profit margin. And at the same time, it wouldn't have been fair to our people to impose unfulfilling work on them. Of the 169, only eight left our company, most of them to serve the client with its new travel partner.

In the end, we survived. Like most humbling experiences, it taught us a great deal and we emerged stronger.

Was what we learned worth an $80 million account? I don't know, but it's certain that we are a better company today. We learned a valuable lesson about paying attention to rumblings in all industries and how they affect our clients. And we strengthened loyalty by showing our people that each individual is important, no matter what obstacles the company faces.

The Food Chain
The Ripple Effects of Corporate Misfortune

Watching your own costs is good business, but it's not enough. You need to keep an eye on the health of companies around you, particularly your clients.

When corporations face economic hardships, when they're faced with slumps in their industry, they're forced to drastically cut expenses. This creates a shock wave up and down the food chain. We can provide the best imaginable service to our clients, but if they have no money to spend, they'll have no choice but to scale back on the business they do with us. When companies cut expenditures, they stop buying computers, office supplies, travel, and so on. Then their suppliers in each of those industries suffer losses, which lead to cutbacks in their companies. Corporate cuts often involve layoffs, or worse yet, insolvency.

No one escapes these troubles. Even if your own house is in order, if your next-door neighbor's house is on fire, yours is in danger too.

What's the answer? I wish I had a cookbook recipe that would make a company immune to the cyclical effects of a downturn in the economy or in its industry. I don't. But we have learned the value of keeping your eyes open to factors that affect not just your own company or industry but all businesses worldwide. Knowing what problems your customers and potential clients might face puts you in the driver's seat.

Look into the Future
The Importance of Forecasting

Don't look back. Something may be gaining on you.

—LEROY "SATCHEL" PAIGE, *Maybe I'll Pitch Forever*

Looking into the future is as important as looking around you. To do so, you have to continually sharpen your ability to think like the marketplace—your clients and competitors. In a way it's like "pirating" the thought processes of those around you. It's an acquired skill that comes with practice.

An admirer once asked Sir Isaac Newton how he was able to make such astonishing discoveries in astronomy. His answer was simply, "By always thinking about them."

We spend a lot of time contemplating the future. When we make a decision, we discuss all the possible outcomes and how they will affect our clients. We debate about what our competitors' next moves will be. When you play the role of another company, its vantage point becomes clearer. By using this process, we've foreseen airline mergers and bankruptcies, personnel changes at the highest levels of corporate America, and trends in both our industry and general consumer demand—all well before they came to be.

Nothing is more thrilling than seeing something you've predicted come true, particularly if you've acted on those projections and positioned your clients and your company for a position of strength in that future. This foresight can be reached through the science of deduction, a sort of industrial logic that comes from experience in the marketplace, open-mindedness, and concentration on what waits beyond the horizon.

Listening skills are important and so is the art of observation—studying how individuals or companies have reacted under similar circumstances. Combine the two with "if/then" logic and trends begin to materialize before your eyes, if you become accustomed to watching for them.

One key to discovering trends is open communication within your organization, particularly among your central team charged with initiating strategic development. In our case, our core of vice presidents meets weekly to review intelligence from the field and play out possible scenarios. We try to think like our clients, then as if we were our competitors, and finally prospective clients. This process has given us a clear competitive advantage.

It's rewarding to be on the cutting edge. It's even more fun if, by the time your competitors hear about what you're doing, you're already doing something else.

Forecasting has to be based partly on history, and mainly on the ability to recognize ways in which the present can be improved. It's important to be in a position to act quickly. Once you uncover a need you have to be ready to jump. By the time buyers and competitors come to see the need, you'll be the only one properly positioned to fill it.

Successful forecasters understand trends. Whether money managers, meteorologists, or bookies, they're able to spot trends while they're embryonic. We call it "educated anticipation," and it has helped us make some of our most successful decisions.

There's a Reason They Call It a "Brave" New World
The Fears and Rewards of Doing Things Differently

Taking an unorthodox approach can be difficult. Doing things differently sometimes brings on more heat. When you do something the traditionally accepted way and it doesn't work, people tend to say you gave it a good shot. But when you try something unusual and it fails, people often say it's because you went out on a limb. It's important for senior management to give people the security to take intelligent chances, letting them know it's all right to fail if the consequences were well thought out.

We all have natural comfort zones, but beyond them lies a world of new opportunities. It's like the saying, "You can't say anything you don't already know." It's a testimony to listening, because only then do we learn anything. The same goes for our actions. If we insist on always doing things the same way, we can't learn anything new, so we limit our results to what they are today.

Light-Years Ahead
What Does the Future Hold?

Some of the most popular movies in recent years have dealt with going back to the past to correct the present or future, like *Terminator I* and *II* and *Back to the Future I* and *II*. The common theme is that what we do today creates tomorrow's world. But we can't go back in time, so we'd better consider the future effects of what we do today.

What will business be like in 1995, 2005, 2015? You have to think about it and do something about it *now*.

Companies will be left behind if they spend all of their time and resources on today, this week, and this year. The lag time between strategy and reality can be lengthy. The only way to ensure success and longevity is to grasp the coming decades, plan for them now, and begin implementing those strategies.

It can be better to make a mistake than to delay acting upon an idea out of fear. Ideas become stale when they are shelved, and so does enthusiasm. That doesn't mean we need to make rash decisions. We need to make wise ones *quickly*.

How can a company spare this much time studying the future? Thinking about the future takes no more time than thinking about the present. While some companies might be thinking about next year, others are thinking about five years from now. In five years, while short-term companies are thinking about the coming year, companies committed to the future will be thinking about five years from that time.

The real challenge is to shift the planning cycle from present to future while succeeding today. The shift requires a certain period of double time, when today and tomorrow must be attended to while planning for the long term. But once a company shifts gears, it's on track for the future.

Even the most thorough planning doesn't guarantee smooth sailing. Every strategic plan has to be built on flexibility to allow for opportunities that present themselves, as well as unanticipated challenges. People need to be able to modify long-standing strategy on a daily basis and fine-tune it to today's application.

Plato told a story of his predecessor, the Greek philosopher Thales (?640–?546 B.C.). It seems he was walking along a road while looking up at the sky, studying the stars, when he fell into a well. A servant girl rescued him and remarked that while he was fascinated with what was in the sky, he failed to see what was under his feet.

While we need to keep tabs on the present, we do have a number of theories about what's in store for us in the future. We're building programs, products, and strategies based upon those forecasts. They include things that hardly seem possible today. But then, decades ago, neither did many of the things we take for granted, such as space travel, personal computers, fax machines, and supersonic travel. The science fiction of today is the reality of tomorrow.

But people are finding themselves with growing demands on their time. They're watching their lives become more complex. As things become increasingly sophisticated, people will be drawn to the basics. So while the new inventions of the future promise to bring on many positive changes in our world, they'll bring with them a renewed desire for the best things in life—nice people, quality, ethics, and trust. The company of the future will master the skill of blending the best of the old and the new.

Looking Around You and Ahead
A Summary

- Be alert to changes all around you, because as unrelated as they may seem, they send ripple effects throughout the "food chain." It's particularly critical to keep an eye on the health of your clients.

- Sharpen your ability to think like the marketplace, your competitors, and your clients. Listen, observe, use deduction, practice spotting trends, and study their origins.

- Hold regular strategy meetings, during which your top leaders review intelligence from the field and play out every possible scenario and its effects on the marketplace and your company.
- Act *today* for the coming years and decades. There's lag time between concept and reality in developing new products and services. If you spent yesterday planning for today, you can spend today preparing for tomorrow.

CHAPTER 13

OPEN PARTNERSHIPS

Dr. David Livingstone, a Scottish medical missionary and explorer, made a trip to Central Africa in 1870 and disappeared. Sir Henry Morton Stanley, explorer and journalist for the *New York Herald,* was commissioned by his publisher to find Dr. Livingstone. After an exhaustive eight-month search, Stanley found Dr. Livingstone in Ujiji on November 10, 1871, and uttered his famous words: "Dr. Livingstone, I presume?" The news made headlines around the world. And after this historic meeting the two explored Africa together.

Not all partnerships begin with such flair, but through the years the world has been better because of partnerships that have produced results individuals couldn't have. Take Rodgers and Hammerstein, for instance. Richard Rodgers composed the music; Oscar Hammerstein wrote the lyrics. Together, they brought us such greats as *Oklahoma!* and *South Pacific* in the 1940s, and they're still popular half a century later. Partnerships like that don't happen every day. They take a little magic, creativity, and trust.

Look at how we're living these days. Alarm systems in our cars and our homes, people creating fortresses like Fort Knox. But most of us long for those days gone by when we could leave our doors unlocked. Everyone knew their neighbors. Business was done on a handshake.

We still cling to that type of relationship. Sure, we have contracts too, but to us the handshake is more important. Maybe it's because our company is one hundred years old and it remembers doing business the old way. Possibly it's because we started as a family business in the business of reuniting families. Or maybe we just forgot to change. But open partnerships are a key to our success.

The climate today far from encourages open partnerships, particularly in our cutthroat industry, which has been marked by razor-thin profit margins, a siege of mergers and acquisitions, business failures, and at times, a lack of professionalism and integrity. However, this environment makes straightforward partnerships more important than ever. Our company may not resemble the storefront business from which it originated, but we've held fast to its turnback principles: trust, honesty, and faithful partnerships.

More can be accomplished when clients and suppliers work together like true partners in a venture. Great things happen when clients look at us as a strategic partner rather than a vendor. Beyond the purchasing of basic products and services lies a world of opportunity to be innovative in defining and filling our clients' needs.

Operating a Nudist Colony
Getting to Really Know Your Client

Fig leaves are banned at our company. We believe there can be nothing that you hide from your clients. It doesn't work anyway: The more you try to hide something, the more curious people become. Figuratively speaking, we operate a nudist colony where every last nook and cranny is bared to our clients.

We've found that openness is reciprocal. The more candid we are with our clients, the more candid they are with us. The level of trust we build is mutual. It's surprisingly comfortable to operate in this environment, and this honest information exchange enables us to do a better job for our clients.

The openness has to start with the sales process. The more up-front a company is about its capabilities, the better its relationship will be with its clients. Everyone knows what to expect. Nobody has to scramble to make things happen. This creates the right fit for long-term partnerships.

Companies can't overlook the importance of supplier relationships in helping to meet their clients' needs. To manufacturing firms who operate "just in time" inventory systems, it's essential their suppliers provide quality products on the date needed. A zero-inventory system can be very effective, but only if the products are there when they need to be handed off from supplier to buyer.

In our case, we rely upon our airline, hotel, and car rental suppliers to provide the end product—the travel itself. We have to assume responsibility for more than just our portion of the service. We need to make sure that our suppliers are performing for our clients.

Part of our quality process is to involve ourselves from

beginning to end of the service process, regardless of where our portion of it officially ends. Many of our service-guarantee refunds have been because of supplier error, but we returned our commissions to our clients because we hold ourselves responsible for the entire process. After taking care of our clients, we can discuss the issue with our suppliers.

Any company could benefit from taking a hard look at its suppliers' businesses. If a company can't manufacture its products on time because of late or defective parts from a supplier, it becomes the company's problem, and ultimately, the client's. Excuses don't work.

One for All and All for One
The Importance of the Three-Way Relationship

We need to work in concert with our clients and suppliers in strategic partnerships. The way we see it, all three parties need to know exactly what to expect. Even in the most delicate arena of all—pricing—we take a very candid approach.

Our industry is very dependent on the price of airfares. Either this can put companies like ours at the mercy of the marketplace, or we can fight to control our own destiny. We have begun working with our clients and key suppliers to change the compensation structure of our industry. The traditional structure pays higher commissions for more expensive tickets, and that goes against every principle we believe in.

We have created programs with a number of our clients that financially reward us for saving them money. We share in the rewards of special fares we negotiate on their behalf.

We think this may be the future of commission-based businesses. It lessens any potential conflict in the client-supplier relationship.

Often, in our industry, pricing is based on what it will take to lure accounts—offering rebates and similar programs. But this type of pricing is deceptive. The fact is that far greater value can be obtained through proactive travel management than rebating. But it's a method of pricing that's offered less frequently and is less understood.

Here's a theoretical example of the difference between the two pricing strategies. Let's say Company A is considering both Travel Agency X and Rosenbluth to manage its $20 million travel account. Travel agency X offers a 2 percent rebate equaling a total of $400,000 in cash back to Company A.

Rebating doesn't help anyone involved. When a service company gives away its commissions, it doesn't leave much to pay its people and to invest in the future. In the end that hurts both the company and its clients. We try to hold firm to a position that makes everyone win.

Our approach is to offer significant savings. We might guarantee the company a $1 million reduction in travel costs through consolidated purchasing, specially negotiated fares, and the manipulation of travel patterns toward less expensive alternatives. In effect, we're saying, "Why assume you have to continue to spend $20 million? Let's reduce that."

How will we do it? We do use our size to negotiate special rates for our clients, but most large companies can do that in their industries. We also take inventory positions to secure the most economical rates for our clients. We study their travel patterns closely and guarantee our suppliers a certain level of business based upon our historical data. Many times we buy rooms and seats in advance for our clients at deeply discounted rates.

The unique value comes from using information creatively. We can tell each of our clients exactly what it costs them to travel between point A and point B at any given time of day, day of week, or week of the year. This information can be used to shift travel patterns to those times during which travel is more economical.

There is a big discrepancy in costs for different days, times, and routes. Why travel on Monday if it costs much more than Wednesday and your meeting is flexible? Why fly during the peak times of day if it isn't necessary, when off-peak costs less and there are fewer crowds to hassle with? People just aren't aware of the opportunities for savings that exist through the power of this type of information.

The key is to share our information with both our clients and our suppliers. We show our suppliers that we are able to shift business to whoever will offer our clients the best rates and services. The suppliers who participate get more business, our clients get significant savings, and we share in those savings.

We operate on the premise that most wise organizations would rather purchase a less expensive airline ticket than a costly one that comes with a rebate. We have the information that makes such savings possible, and rather than keep it to ourselves, we share it with our clients and help them use it to their advantage.

Which program will Company A select? We find that most often companies prefer our approach. But believe it or not, many are blinded by the glare of the rebate and will forgo $1 million in savings to have a $400,000 check in hand. When asked how they could make that choice we've had some prospective clients tell us that savings are realized by the company as a whole, but when a check comes in, their particular department receives the credit for that income.

While in most cases this approach results in less benefit to the company, it's sometimes a fact of life. We've seen this type of practice diminish some in recent years and hopefully that will continue. The savings approach will usually win in the end.

Have we ever been burned by taking this direction? A couple of times. But when you operate ethically, people will usually come to your aid. A few years ago that's just what happened when someone tried to cut us out of the loop.

We have a long-standing client with whom we have developed some of our most creative and forward-thinking programs. The company appointed a new person to oversee travel who proved to be more interested in short-term gains than long-term opportunities. We shaped a new plan to capture additional savings for this client, and the strategy included a key supplier. After we presented our plan to the client, he went directly to the supplier and tried to renegotiate an arrangement including only their two companies so he could keep all of the savings. But our supplier had the long term in mind. He declined, and called to let us know what had happened.

We shied away from creating this type of open program with that particular client for a while, but after a short time, he moved on. Another travel administrator is on board there now, and together with him and our trusted supplier we continue to shape savings programs that include everyone.

Are You Your Client's Customer?
The Importance of Supporting Your Clients

We're all so busy concentrating on providing our clients with the products and services we offer that sometimes we don't see the most basic way to serve our clients—by being their customers.

We have a policy at Rosenbluth to utilize the products and services of our clients whenever feasible. We manage the travel account of Carnation, so we naturally use Coffee-mate in all of our offices. Gillette is a client of ours, so we use Paper Mate pens, which they manufacture.

Since Kodak is our client, we use Kodak film, slides, and equipment for our presentations. Because The Scott Company and James River Corporation are our clients, we use only their paper products. Each time we visit the rest room, we're reminded of how important our clients' products are.

We insist on Stainmaster carpets in our offices, because Du Pont is our client. We don't often have the opportunity to use Binney & Smith's Crayolas at work, but they're our client too. So when we asked clients and associates to draw what Rosenbluth meant to them, that's what we sent. Our clients manufacture hundreds of products, and our people know to use them exclusively.

Not only does it support our clients, it helps us to understand them better. We make it a point to learn their businesses. We research the products they make so we can incorporate them into our everyday use.

Welcome Home
Creating an Open Atmosphere

We feel that our business should be like home to our clients. They are welcome at any time, in any of our locations. After all, we're working for them.

No one who's expecting company keeps a messy house or has empty cupboards. Homes in which people are welcome are always clean and hospitable. Offices should be no different.

I had an eye-opening experience a few years ago in one of our vacation locations. I stopped by the office, unannounced, and what I found was an absolute embarrassment. There were half-empty boxes of travel brochures, half-completed reservations on desktops, with atlases open and resource manuals askew. While it sounds productive, and might possibly have been, the sight really disturbed me.

When you go to the dentist, do you want to see used instruments? When you visit your tax specialist, do you want other people's W-2 forms lying around precariously? When you dine in a restaurant do you want to sit down to someone else's half-eaten food? You'd never stand for it.

The same goes for travel. It's a very personal business that takes attention to detail. It's not enough just to be organized—you have to *look* organized. Everyone at Rosenbluth knows this is important to our clients' level of comfort.

What did I do about the chaos in our office? The only thing I felt was right. I asked our clients to leave. I inquired where each was planning to go on their vacation and provided their trips free of charge, explaining that I had some business to discuss with my associates. I locked the door and had a talk with everyone in that office about the importance of keeping their workplace a home, to which our clients will be drawn and will feel both comfortable and welcome.

Afterward, we straightened up the office together for the rest of the day, making it a place we'd want to go. That particular site used to be one of my least favorite, but now it ranks up there with the best of them. Not only have they improved the appearance of their surroundings, but when you look good you feel good. Their productivity has been enhanced and I believe they are happier in their work. I know our clients are happier.

Bringing Clients into the Kitchen
No Areas Should Be "Off Limits" to Clients

Have you ever enjoyed a restaurant until you took a look at the kitchen? More often than not, you're truly disgusted when you catch sight of the kitchen and its operations. Rarely are they very clean, and somehow the food loses its appeal when you see it being prepared.

We try to make a journey into our "kitchen" create a stronger impression than a view from the outside. We work hard to come out ahead in comparisons between our kitchen and the others in our industry. We do know that one rule holds true: When we bring a potential client in to inspect the inner workings of our company, we almost always make the sale.

We encourage current and prospective clients to visit our offices, to see what we're up to and to meet our people. It's common on a typical day for clients to be circulating through our offices, visiting with our associates alongside prospective clients. Our people are comfortable with both their work and our customers, so it's never disruptive. It's just one more way to strengthen the bonds we have with our clients.

Corporate Marriage
The Ultimate Client-Supplier Relationship

The ultimate level in partnership is the fusion of talents. We call it "corporate marriage," and it's the definitive client relationship. What are we talking about? A form of interchange that takes place in an environment of complete trust. An exchange of people.

Technology specialists know information systems. Human resource experts know personnel issues. Operations people know procedure, process, and efficiency. A great deal can be shared across industries. It may be a meeting between counterparts for a day or an associate exchange for a week, a month, or even a year.

These exchanges provide insight into the needs of our clients that can't be attained any other way. The benefits are reciprocal. Our clients who participate in this degree of partnership come to understand more fully the basis from which we work. They understand the objectives we must achieve as a business and the challenges we face in doing so. A walk in each other's shoes builds the platform for true teamwork.

We've learned a great deal from our clients, and I'm proud to say they've learned from us too. The best part of all is that it becomes almost impossible for competitors to try to snatch away any client with whom we have cultivated this level of partnership. As in a good marriage, the commitment is for the duration. There is no need to hold back, and because of that, things can be accomplished that before were thought to be impossible.

Basic relationships will produce basic results. When partners open up to a new level of trust, they reach a plane of creativity in which together they can recreate the marketplace.

The Three R's
The Best Way to Find Good Partners Is to Be One

We all learned in school the fundamental "three R's" that make up the foundation upon which we learn the rest of our lives. Rosenbluth's three R's are just as fundamental to our success as a company: relationships, reputation, and references. We know these are the factors that draw both associates and clients to our company.

I've talked about relationships, but reputation and references are also crucial. Any company can advertise its service, but what really counts is what clients have to say about it. That's reputation. The secret is to translate reputation into references.

Our clients are our best salespeople. When they do the bragging about us, people listen. Most of our clients are happy to discuss our service with prospective clients. The references they have given have made all the difference in the world to our sales efforts. When we and our clients truly see each other as partners, great things happen.

Framework for Open Partnerships
A *Summary*

- Build open partnerships with your own people, your clients, and the suppliers who affect your ability to provide service to your clients. It's the only way to ensure that all concerned will "buy in" to your company's goals and objectives. Empower them with the information necessary to help you succeed.

- Operate your company like a "nudist colony" where you hide nothing from your clients. They will quickly feel comfortable being just as open with you. This straightforward environment has to begin with the sales process and continue through to the end of each transaction, including your suppliers' part in what you do.

   Candid partnerships with suppliers are just as important. They make your work possible. Your clients' perception of your service can hinge upon your suppliers' ability to deliver the services and tools you need to get the job done. Bringing your suppliers into the loop is critical.

- Make your business a home away from home for your clients. Encourage them to visit often and mingle with your people. It'll deepen your relationship. Make sure that every day in every location, you can be proud to host your clients in your offices.

- Bring your clients "into the kitchen." Let them in on your strategy, your goals and objectives. They'll see their role in your long-range plans.

- Know the true value of your products and services and sell based on that value. Don't fall prey to offering flashy pricing to get business. Go for long-term relationships that benefit everyone equitably. That's the way to ensure staying power.

- Reward savings for the company as a whole rather than individual departments bringing in rebate checks. The savings will almost always outweigh a one-time signing bonus.

- Make it company policy to use the products of your clients and let them know. It increases your people's knowledge about your clients, it helps your clients' sales, and it further cements your relationships.

- Consider an exchange program with your clients. Your marketing people should work with theirs, their technology people with yours, and so on. Not only are you sharing ideas and learning new ways of doing things, but it'll put your clients out of your competitors' reach.

- References are essential sales tools and your clients should be your best salespeople. Cultivate your client partnerships and utilize them as references. Continually ensuring client satisfaction will not only help you keep the customers you already have, it'll also reward you with new business.

CHAPTER 14

BLAZING NEW TRAILS

The French classical painter Nicolas Poussin became exasperated when he failed to create the image of foam at the mouth of a spirited horse he had painted. He dashed his sponge against the canvas, and the result was exactly what he had struggled so tediously to produce.

One of the best partnerships we ever forged was a similar case of serendipity. Sometimes an idea just shines for you like a distant light you can't ignore. Our operation in a sleepy farm town was one such light, and its benefits to our company have been astounding.

We've stumbled upon an answer to so many concerns—not just of our company, but of all companies: finding, retaining, and continually motivating the finest people. The answer lies in partnerships between corporate and rural America. Through ours, we have eliminated overtime and temporary work, lowered our operating costs, found an untapped human resource, and branched into a new line of business.

From Cows to Computers
An Offbeat Idea That Changed Our Company

One day in the summer of 1988, my wife and I were discussing the fact that we were expecting rain in Philadelphia for the fifth straight day in a row. Then we got on the subject of the serious drought in the Midwest, and we wished we could send some of our rain their way.

The next day, my associates and I were talking about what we *could* do to help, and the series of events that followed made a real difference in our company. We decided to open a temporary office in the heart of the drought country to provide employment until the drought subsided.

The saying goes, "Give a man a fish and he eats for a day; teach a man to fish and he has food for life." We decided that rather than contribute to a drought relief fund, we'd offer to teach skills that people could use to lessen their dependence upon farming, in which success is contingent upon Mother Nature's cooperation.

We contacted the U.S. Department of Agriculture to ask which state had been the hardest hit, and the answer was North Dakota. We visited the state and asked which area had been most negatively affected, and were told about Linton, a town of about one thousand people. This community was almost totally dependent upon agriculture for its livelihood, and it was here that the drought had been most merciless.

Off we went to Linton. The local economic development group helped us to locate an old tractor implement shop where part of the space was not being utilized. The next day we ran a small "help wanted" ad in the local paper, the *Emmons County Record*, for twenty full-time positions for a three-month period.

From that one mention in the local paper, eighty people showed up the next morning looking for work. So we decided to hire forty part-time people instead of twenty full-time, in order to have a positive impact on more families. We installed computers in our makeshift work space, brought in a team of trainers, and set up shop.

Everyone in the company was asked to submit ideas for work that could be done in our rural office. We studied the type of work that was being done on an overtime basis or by temporary help. It was almost exclusively data entry and other work that was ideal for our new associates.

We came to rely more and more on that office for all types of work, and we noticed that overtime and temporary help in our offices across the country ceased. The alternative became our Linton associates, and we began to wonder how we ever survived without them.

We faced some skepticism. In our own industry, a lot of people thought we had lost our minds. Even in Linton, at first, people wondered why we were there and what we hoped to gain from it. In the beginning we didn't expect to gain anything from it, but the benefits began to unfold.

In just the first few weeks, we began to see a pattern of quality work, with no absenteeism and no turnover. The scope of our new associates' work expanded along with their productivity. Morale was high and that office was the epitome of teamwork.

When we opened there, we hadn't expected benefits to our bottom line, but they were unmistakable. Operating costs are notably lower in rural America, and because the cost of living is so much less than in major metropolitan areas, the salaries are typically lower. You don't see the salary scuffles over highly qualified people that take place in larger cities. Add to that the costs that can be saved by eliminating overtime and temporary work, and you begin to see that doing business in rural America is a sound alternative.

These are just the *financial* benefits to corporations utilizing rural America as a viable option in human resources. Companies may find themselves looking to farm towns simply to find available quality people in the coming years.

Forecast: A National Drought
The Impending Need for Quality People

Our nation will face a human resource crisis in the coming decades. The labor force is shrinking and the demands of corporate America are growing. We'll feel the effects in the future.

The population is aging. Concurrently, the number of people entering the work force under the age of thirty has decreased since 1980 and is expected to continue to decline well into the next millennium. There are concerns over the decline in basic skills our youth possess.

More alternative labor sources are being utilized, and this leaves fewer to call upon in the future. Human resources are the single highest cost item for many American corporations. And people make companies what they are. There is no more important corporate concern for the future.

An Unsheathed Weapon
A Human Resource Solution for the Future

For the most part, corporate and rural America lead separate lives. Sure, we need the products and services that each of us manufactures, but when it comes to business, we don't work as a team. Farmers try to make a living from the land, confronting all the unpredictable forces of nature in the process. American corporations struggle to compete in a fast-moving international arena where they don't enjoy the clear dominance they once did.

Rural America offers a wealth of human resources, not just in sheer numbers but in extraordinary quality and work ethic. The ultimate weapon for corporate America is a double-barreled gun: high quality with low operating costs. It can be found in rural America.

Bringing work from corporate America into rural communities lessens their dependency upon agriculture. This allows people to continue farming, because they are better able to withstand its ups and downs.

I'll Place My Bet on the Farmer
Farming and Business Have More in Common Than You May Realize

The celebrated lawyer Clarence Darrow, who was defense attorney in the historic Scopes trial, was once being interviewed for a magazine article on secrets to success. The interviewer said, "Most of the men I've spoken to so far attribute their success to hard work."

Clarence Darrow replied, "I guess that applies to me, too. I was brought up on a farm. One very hot day I was distributing and packing down the hay which a stacker was constantly dumping on top of me. By noon I was completely exhausted. That afternoon I left the farm, never to return, and I haven't done a day of hard work since."

I don't mean to imply that if you don't come from a farm you don't know how to work, but that there are certain parallels between farming and business. The resourcefulness it takes to run a farm at times exceeds that required for a business. Struggling with nature is no easy task. The days are longer than those of a driven corporate executive. A day on the farm normally begins at 5:00 A.M., but you won't find too many farmers calling it a day at 5:00 P.M.

Farming is teamwork personified. No one can run a farm alone. The land and animals have to be tended daily. There's no such thing as a weekend, holiday, or sick day on a farm. The only option is to cooperate with friend and neighbor to get the job done. And the quality that goes into the making of the product becomes clear at harvest or cattle auction time.

These solid values are learned at an early age on the farm. Most kids put in a full day's work on their family's farm in the hours before and after school. Contrast this inherent work ethic with the challenges companies face in motivating people and the application of the comparisons between business and farming becomes clear.

A Part of the Family
Planting Permanent Roots in Rural America

As I've discussed, we go through countless interviews each year to find the right people. We search far and wide for the cream of the crop and we've been able to find them, but it takes a lot of hard work. What we've found in rural America is an abundance of the type of person we look for, and that's rare.

So after just six weeks, we decided to make our rural office a permanent one. We announced our plans during the final session of our company-wide meeting, and the announcement was met with few dry eyes. Every one of our people had been touched by our Linton associates in some way, whether through the quality of their work, their can-do attitude, or their contagious enthusiasm. This was a clear instance of a decision that was good business and the right thing to do.

Today we have over 150 full-time associates in our North Dakota office. Data entry is still a part of their work, but they also take travel reservations, deal with much of our accounting work, and handle our entire customer service operation.

Home on the Range
The Story of a Very Special Place

Happy the man who far from schemes of business, like the early generations of mankind, works his ancestral acres with oxen of his own breeding, from all usury free.

—HORACE (65–8 B.C.)

In 1989 we held a strategic planning meeting in Linton (the one I discussed earlier, when I talked about our fence-building exercise). We stayed at a roadside motel, held our meetings in the local electric cooperative building, and instead of playing golf or skiing for recreation, we rode horses and did farm chores. It was the best meeting we ever had.

We found ourselves doing everything as a group, not breaking into foursomes. Everyone felt unrestrained, renewed, creative. We came back a stronger team. Every strategic meeting since then has been held in North Dakota.

From the beginning of time, man worked with the land. Only since the turn of the century have people become disconnected from it. Something natural has been lost in urban life that can be recaptured on a farm.

We decided the experience was worth sharing with other companies, so we bought a thousand acres of rolling prairieland and built a place like no other. We call it "The Rivery," and it's a ranch where companies can hold small meetings in seclusion—one group at a time. We designed The Rivery based on trust. There are no cash registers. We operate on the honor system. Most of our guests leave their doors open. The kitchen and the bar are open twenty-four hours a day, so guests can help themselves to whatever they'd like whenever they want. Accommodations, meals, and many activities are part of the all-inclusive package. Our guests help themselves to any additional activities or amenities and simply notify us afterward. Charges are billed so our guests don't have to worry about it while they're enjoying their stay.

The Rivery specializes in creating out-of-the-ordinary experiences, like meetings in a one-room schoolhouse or out under the open skies, perched on bales of hay. There are rodeos, cattle drives, and trail rides. It's an unusual blend of rusticity and elegance.

Each day our guests are served afternoon tea, and turn-down service includes freshly baked warm cookies and ice-cold milk. There are no room numbers and there's no check-in or check-out process. Every staff member knows each guest's name.

Our staff is made up of local farmers, trained by the Ritz-Carlton organization in the art of hospitality. Our clients say we've created a place that embodies the spirit of the heartland, and we're proud of that. We've been sending our clients to resorts for a century—why not our own? And what better place to build it than the place we think will play a big part in our future?

All Across America
Exploring Rural Opportunities for Your Company

A few months ago, I gave a speech to a group of teachers from rural communities and was asked if we planned to expand our rural operations. I replied that I hoped we would have the opportunity to do so someday.

A news wire picked up parts of the presentation, and over the following few weeks I received information from literally hundreds of small farm towns across the nation inviting us to become a part of their communities. When we do decide to grow, we'll face a tough choice.

There are "Lintons" all across America, ripe for partnerships with corporations. The diversity of industry offered to rural America will save our nation's farming communities. The wealth of affordable, quality human resources will help our nation get back into the competitive ring.

Companies have come to realize that so many types of work know no geographical boundaries. When you call a company to order merchandise or speak with a customer service department, do you know or even care where your call is being answered?

It doesn't matter where the call originates. What most people want to know is that their merchandise order or customer service request is being handled expertly and courteously. Companies are beginning to appreciate that, and we've been inundated with calls from corporations interested in what we've done in rural North Dakota.

Our clients became interested in the feasibility of such an operation for their own companies because of the work done on their behalf in Linton. Then nonclient companies began to call us about it. We now regularly take executives from organizations far and wide to see our Linton office. We share information on how we established the office and put them in touch with people who can help them get started.

Just a year and a half ago, a large East Coast HMO accompanied us on one of our trips, and within a couple of months they hired over three hundred people in a town not far from our North Dakota site. They have since expanded their operation. Several firms who contacted us have opened similar facilities, including a hotel reservations company and a telemarketing firm that located in small North Dakota communities, and a large airline's frequent flyer tracking operation, which is now located in South Dakota.

Through our office in Linton and our introduction of the concept of rural and corporate partnerships, we have benefited our clients in an unconventional and unexpected way. And we have picked up a few new clients along the way.

The Rural Route
A *Summary*

- Pursue an idea if you believe in it, no matter how absurd it might seem to the outside world. That's how most revolutionary ideas are born.

- Search for pockets of people who fit your company's culture and work ethic. We have found ours in rural America.

- Ready your company for a drought in human resources that will be brought about by a number of factors. Our nation is growing older, basic skills are declining; more alternative labor sources are being utilized, which all leads up to fewer untapped human resources as we enter the increasingly competitive future.

- Consider rural America as a weapon for global competitiveness. The combination of high quality and reasonable operating costs is hard to beat.

- If you are interested in exploring your options in rural America, our company would be more than happy to help you in any way we can, including providing information we have gained through our experience there and the experiences of the companies we have helped to establish rural operations.

CHAPTER 15

A LOT TO DIGEST

I've made some statements in this book that might seem strange to a lot of people. Things like "The customer can no longer come first." If you were to look at that statement alone it could be alarming. But when you explain why it works it's as comforting as a hug.

I want to bring it all together, so you can see it as a trail to a different way of doing business—a way that has worked for us and can work for any company that's willing to try it.

First impressions are lasting. Most people spend their first days on a new job filling out forms. But the beginning of a career should be an event to remember. A creative and inspiring orientation program gets everyone in step, instills culture, and builds loyalty—rewards that will repay a company time and again.

Happiness in the workplace is a strategic advantage. Service comes from the heart, and people who feel cared for will care more. Unhappiness results in error, turnover, and other evils. To strengthen happiness you have to measure it—using Crayolas, voice mail, it doesn't matter as long as you gauge it. Finally, companies have to have fun. When was the last time you excelled at something you disliked?

Inventing the future is a matter of seeking opportunities to capitalize on change, and being ready to seize them. Before a company can do that, it must be free of undue dependence upon outside parties and prepared to manage the impending growth.

Finding the right people takes a broad view, looking beyond the standard sources of your industry. People should be selected as much for team fit as individual contribution. They should be interviewed not only by their potential leaders, but by those whom they will lead and their peers. The interviewing process should be unusual because you can tell more about a person when his or her guard is down. But above all, look for nice people.

Perpetual training is a secret weapon, because the growth of a company is really just the aggregate of the growth of its people. Broad-based programs that are philosophical in nature are as important as technical training. It all starts with the very first day of work—people should be initiated in the company with an orientation they'll never forget. And training should be offered to everyone throughout their careers.

Technology is a tool that can reduce stress and improve service. It can automate mundane processes, leaving people free to concentrate on the more creative and personal aspects of service. The best technology tools are built based upon the input of the people who will use them. This also incorporates the technology group into the company's mainstream.

Service is an attitude, an art, and a process, and we're all in the service business no matter what our industry is. When you're in tune with your clients, you feel service in your gut. That's attitude. Art comes from caring and creativity. And process comes from a quality initiative. But it has to be the right one for your company because if it's not, process can get in the way of progress.

Culture defines every organization. It's important for companies to capture the concept of what they'd like theirs to say, formalize it, share it with their people, and celebrate it. But the secret to culture is sincerity, for without the actions to go with the words, they're empty.

The birth and nurturing of ideas has to be taken seriously. Innovation will be encouraged in an environment of creativity and freedom. Studying the origin of ideas can spark the process. They can come from the desire to do something better, a problem that needs solving, or from almost anywhere. Ideas need to be protected, but they become stronger when they are tested.

The gardening process is important, because after all that work finding the right people you need to help keep them that way. Make sure politics doesn't work in your organization. Reward those who are contributing and not seeking recognition, those who help others succeed. Break down barriers by moving people around and cross-training them. People should be reviewed by those they lead as well as those who lead them.

Look around you and up ahead, because it's not enough just to mind your own company and industry. The health of surrounding industries can have a ripple effect, particularly the industries of clients. But it's just as important to look into the future by thinking like the marketplace. It'll prepare you to proactively serve your clients and to outwit your competitors.

Open partnerships make a higher level of relationship

possible with your clients. Your offices should remain welcome homes to them. They should be invited into the kitchen to inspect the ingredients of your product. Your clients should be your best salespeople. And you should be their customer.

Blazing new trails means pursuing what you believe in no matter what anyone else thinks. By locating in a farm town we discovered a gold mine. The people there are our answer to the human resource drought. It could be your answer too.

A DISTANCE TO GO

We're confident in what we believe and secure in sharing it with you. But that doesn't mean we always live up to our expectations. While most of the principles and programs I've discussed here are daily practice, some still remain aspirations. I think it's important to tell you that we're not completely there yet but we're getting close. I hope that putting these beliefs in writing will help both you and us.

Rosenbluth International
2401 Walnut
Philadelphia, PA 19103

NOTES gl.

Page 25 Nancy K. Austin, "Wacky Management Ideas That Work," *Working Woman*, November 1991.

Page 92 Tom Peters, *On Achieving Excellence*, copyright © 1988 by TPG Communications. All rights reserved. Reprinted with permission.

Page 146 Richard Borden, *Public Speaking as Listeners Like It!* (New York: Harper & Brothers, 1935).

Page 147 Robert Frost, "The Road Not Taken," in *Mountain Interval* (New York: Henry Holt & Company, 1916).

Page 156 Adapted and reprinted by permission from *The American Heritage Dictionary of the English Language*, copyright © 1981 by Houghton Mifflin Company.

Page 174 Excerpt from *The Little Prince* by Antoine de Saint-Exupéry, copyright © 1971 by Harcourt Brace Jovanovich, Inc., reprinted by permission of the author.

Page 176   Michael Hammer, "Reengineering Work: Don't Automate, Obliterate," *Harvard Business Review*, July–August 1990.

Page 194   From *Maybe I'll Pitch Forever*, copyright © 1962 by David Lipman. Reprinted by permission of McIntosh and Otis, Inc.

Page 218   Arnold Packer and William Johnston, *Workforce 2000* (Indianapolis, Ind.: Hudson Institute, 1987).

Pages 219   Excerpt from *Fair Fights and Foul: A Dissenting Law-*
   –220   *yer's Life*, copyright © 1965 by Thurman Arnold, reprinted by permission of Harcourt Brace Jovanovich, Inc.

BIBLIOGRAPHY

Arnold, Thurman. *Fair Fights and Foul: A Dissenting Lawyer's Life.* Orlando, Fla.: Harcourt Brace Jovanovich, 1965.

Austin, Nancy K. "Wacky Management Ideas That Work," *Working Woman,* November 1991.

Bartlett, John. *Bartlett's Familiar Quotations.* Boston: Little, Brown and Company, 1980.

Borden, Richard. *Speaking as Listeners Like It!* New York: Harper & Brothers, 1935.

Fadiman, Clifton. *The Little, Brown Book of Anecdotes.* Boston: Little, Brown and Company, 1985.

Frost, Robert. "The Road Not Taken," in *Mountain Interval.* New York: Henry Holt & Company, 1916.

Hammer, Michael. "Reengineering Work: Don't Automate, Obliterate," *Harvard Business Review,* July–August 1990.

Lipman, David. *Maybe I'll Pitch Forever.* New York: Bantam, Doubleday, Dell, 1961.

Packer, Arnold, and William Johnston. *Workforce 2000.* Indianapolis, Ind.: Hudson Institute, 1987.

Peters, Tom. *On Achieving Excellence.* Palo Alto, Calif.: TPG Communications, December 1988.

Saint-Exupéry, Antoine de. *The Little Prince.* Orlando, Fla.: Harcourt Brace Jovanovich, 1971.

INDEX